Your Religion Is

Also by Joel Grus:

YOUR RELIGION IS FALSE

JOEL GRUS

Brightwalton

Your Religion Is False

Published by Brightwalton LLC
Seattle, Washington
brightwalton.com

ISBN-10: 0-9824818-0-2
ISBN-13: 978-0-9824818-0-6

Contents

RELIGIONS FOUNDED BY MOHAMMED   118

RELIGIONS THAT MAY OR MAY NOT BE CHRISTIANITY, DEPENDING ON WHOM YOU ASK   134

RELIGIONS POPULAR WITH FLAKEY CALIFORNIANS AND REBELLIOUS TEENAGERS   151

The secret to success is to offend the greatest number of people.

George Bernard Shaw

Preface

Your religion is false.

When my (now) editor telephoned me, suggesting this topic for a book, my first reaction was that it seemed a bit ambitious. Why not, I asked her, start with a less-sweeping thesis, like "Zoroastrianism is Probably Not The One True Faith," or "A Few Minor Points the Rabbis Got Wrong," or "At the Center of the Catholic Church Lies a Murderous Conspiracy That Only Tom Hanks Can Uncover and Defeat"?

Someone named Dan Brown, she informed me, had already written on my Zoroastrianism idea, and Simon and Schuster (Jews both) would never allow such an overtly anti-Rabbinic book to be published. In addition, she continued, the publishing world was currently enthralled by what she called "The New Atheism," a concerted push by Communists (though she never explicitly identified them as such) and creators of vampire-themed young-adult detective novels (like *Nancy Drew Blood*) to purge the bestseller lists of religious mainstays like *The Bible, Chicken Soup for the Zoroastrian's Soul*, and *Awaken the Giant Within*, in order to make room for a new generation of heathen authors. A book like *Your Religion Is False* could be "publishing gold," she concluded, and could help her eradicate some of her payday-loan debt.

But why me, I objected? After all, I was kicked out of bartending school for plagiarism (my "Manhattan" tasted too similar to Woody Allen's to be coincidence, the dean decided), and I had been forced to put my Broadway adaptation of *Revenge of the Nerds* on indefinite hiatus once I realized I couldn't figure out the right melody for the song "That's My Pi," and the one time I worked up the courage to post one of my Snape-on-Dumbledore slashfic stories ("The Chamber of Secrets We're Not Supposed to Tell Grown-ups About") to the internet, it was deemed both derivative and insufficiently erotic by the other members of the "mug holes" online community.

Here my sweet editor was nothing but encouraging. She'd chosen me, she said, on the basis of a series of letters I'd written to the local paper, complaining about their weekly syndicated column "Ask Reverend Bill," whose eponymous author regularly exhorted the few of us who read all the way through to page L22 to accept Jesus Christ as our savior. "This is valuable news-space," I suggested in a representative letter, "that could be more profitably used for Japanese number puzzles, or to give movie actors a forum in which to advise us on the optimal play of card games, or for the world's smartest woman (assuming we can identify and locate her and that she speaks English) to answer questions about mathematics and how best to live our lives." Every week another column explaining the supposed virtues and peeves of the reverend's triune man-god, every week a new letter to the paper, eventually transcribed to the web and indexed by Google and subsequently located by my editor. (I did not think to ask which search terms she had used, though now I wish I had.)

Nonetheless, I'd never written a book before. She had an answer for this, too: "Do you think Richard Dawkins ever wrote anything before *The God Delusion*? Christopher Hitchens before *God is Not Great*?" As these were posed as questions (which I was unable to answer on account of my unfamiliarity with either man), her response was not technically a lie, and this technical non-lie provided me much of the motivation I needed to finish this project, at which point I visited a library and found that both men had in fact written several books, strangely all about the crimes of the Clinton family: *No One Left to Lie To*, *The Mysterious Life and Death of Vince Foster*, and *I'm Not Saying the Clintons are Criminals But I'm Not Saying They're Not*, among others. So I called up my editor and asked her whether I should travel back in time and write a book in this genre to pre-establish my credentials (I had the title "Chelsea's White Slavery Ring" all picked out); however, she started to lecture me on laws of thermodynamics and faster-than-light travel and the grandfather paradox, and eventually I hung up the phone and went back down to my underground bunker, where I stacked gold ingots and checked sacks of wheat for grain weevils and waited for the royalty checks to start arriving.

But I'm getting ahead of myself. To write about your religion, I needed to learn about your religion. And so I began my research. I underwent the training to join the *Corpo della Gendarmeria*, the police force of the Vatican, during which I routinely tricked my superiors into visiting a leather bar in Rome, made unnervingly-realistic sound effects with my mouth, and attempted to seduce fellow cadet Kim Cattrall. I scoured the papers of the world for offensive cartoons and delivered death threats to their cartoonists (ironically, this led to a prolonged correspondence and eventual friendship with Brad Anderson, creator of *Marmaduke*). I visited several psychics, who predicted (individually) that I would someday find love with an actress several years my senior, that I would never find love, and that the greatest love of all was already inside of me. I learned and practiced the basics of *schechita*, Kosher ritual slaughter, until a kind man from animal control (whom my kind neighbors had thoughtfully invited) came into my backyard mid-bloodletting and asked in the politest possible way (certainly without threatening me with jail time) that I stop.

I read the entire *Mission Earth* dekalogy, the *Left Behind* series, the *Ender's Game* trilogy, and the *Kama Sutra*. I watched *Yentl, Pulp Fiction, The Craft*, several episodes of "Highway to Heaven," and the entire third season of "Charles in Charge." I purchased and studied a fan-compiled, questionably-legal videocassette of *WWF Classics: Best of the Iron Sheikh*. I skipped several Sundays of "Breakfast with the Beatles," months of "Classic Rock Block Party Weekends," and many mornings of Rush Limbaugh so that I could listen to religious programs like "Father Kresta's Daily Pro-Life Harangue" and "WAHY: Your Station For Ululation" and "Michael Medved Applies Naggy Conservative Judaism to Movies and Politics." I practiced vegetarianism (and occasionally veganism) for several hours every morning and several hours again each night. I ate cases and cases of fortune cookies and analyzed every prediction within for truth and relevance, both with and without "in bed" appended. I observed thousands of circumcisions, some in person and many more over the internet. I prayed as fervently as I knew how: "Please, god, make Jeter strike out!" "Please, god, let Jeter drop this popup, and also, if it's not too much to ask, can you suspend the laws of nature so that the infield fly rule doesn't apply?" "Please, god, give Jeter herpes!"

And while none of these prayers came true (except maybe for the herpes, which I have no easy way of checking), I like to think that these explorations gave me key insights into your religion, and that you and I are brothers (or sisters) in our faith. Which is why I feel a mild sadness (counterbalanced by a giddy excitement) over informing you that your religion is false.

However, it may make you feel better to know that, in order to avoid being accused of false advertising by your differently-religious neighbor who might also pick up this book (that's right, I know all about your differently-religious neighbor and how he goes through your books), I have devoted large sections of the book to explaining why *every other religion besides yours is false*, which presumably is something you fervently believe already and are eager for me to justify. With such common cause, I can only assume that you are as excited as I am about proceeding.

THE FUNDAMENTALS OF WHY YOUR RELIGION IS FALSE

I

The basics of religion

Unless you are reading this in North Korea (where, I understand from watching "The 700 Club," traditional religions like Christianity and Zoroastrianism have largely been replaced with something called Juche, whose rituals involve starving and listening to government-run radio stations), you are probably familiar with religion, although – depending on your circumstances – you may know it as "why daddy is required to hit me with a brass fireplace poker when I fail to show him proper amounts of respect" or "those expensive skin-galvanometer sessions I submit to in order to further my show-business career" or "the reason the beautiful, beautiful act of a man making love to another man is in fact 'an abomination.'"

But if I asked you to define it, could you? If you're anything like me, you've probably been staring out the window for the last half hour, watching a squirrel run back and forth and back and forth on a branch, until you realized that you had no idea what the definition of religion was and decided that you were just going to cut and paste from Wikipedia:

> A **religion** is a set of beliefs and practices, often centered upon specific supernatural and moral claims about reality, the cosmos, and human nature, and often codified as prayer, ritual, and religious law. Religion also encompasses ancestral or cultural traditions, writings, history, and mythology, as well as personal faith and mystic experience. The term "religion" refers to both the personal practices related to communal faith and to group rituals and communication stemming from shared conviction.

As this definition represents the collaborative effort of Wikipedians with trust-inspiring names like "Wolfdog" and "Jeff3000" and "Pharmboy" and "Universal Hero," I have little choice but to consider it authoritative. Nonetheless, I find it unsatisfyingly vague.

For instance, National League Baseball is a set of beliefs (e.g. "The pitcher ought to bat for himself") and practices (e.g. the sacrifice bunt), centered on supernatural (e.g. "God hates the Mets") and moral (e.g. "Kill the umpire!") claims, encompassing traditions (e.g. "Oh Boy! Oberto Free Summer Sausage Night"), writings (e.g. *Merkle's Ninth-Inning Boner*), history (e.g. the "spitball patent" controversy) and mythology (e.g. the legend of a hyperkinetic, man-sized Chicken who haunts San Diego). However, despite the best efforts of my college roommate, who used to spend his summers attending Atlanta Braves games in ritual headdress and war-paint, waving a tomahawk and chanting "Strikum Out! Strikum Out!" with comically-stiff diction, scholars generally do not consider baseball a religion, in the way that, say, soccer is.

What makes a religion?

To add some crispness to the definition, I walked over to Safeway to conduct some "man on the street" interviews. Before the manager pointed me to a "NO SOLICITING" sign and escorted me from the premises, I managed to collect a wide variety of responses to my question "what makes a religion?" (The most common response, "what makes a religion what?" was discarded for being unhelpful.) A handful of answers came up over and over again:

- worship of giant stone heads
- comforting unconditional love of invisible sky-man
- arbitrary dietary rules
- opposition to science
- menstrual blood considered "dirty"
- self-flagellation
- reverence of the prophet Zoroaster
- infallibility of book written centuries ago by cave people
- blissful afterlife for top donors

Regardless of the religion you profess, some of the above should look familiar to you.

Because different religions have so many commonalities, some scientists believe that religion is itself a natural phenomenon, and that we should see similar patterns of behavior in other species. (It turns out that most of these scientists are zoologists who study either the Praying Mantis, the Jerusalem Cricket, the Monkfish, the Saint Bernard, or the Mohammedan Terrier, although this may just be a happy coincidence.) In any event, it is worth investigating what we can learn about the origins of religion.

2

The origins of religion

Although written records from more than 40 years ago are scarce (at least at the library closest to my house), archaeologists excavating sites where early humans lived have found a variety of religious artifacts, including bones, dirt, arrowheads, pottery shards, and fossilized tortillas with Virgin-Mary-shaped bake marks. After careful study, scholars have concluded that the earliest religions were little more than collections of rituals and stories intended to explain phenomena that primitive man was incapable of understanding, to add a false veneer of "meaning" to what must have been difficult lives, and to help tribal leaders legitimize their authority and control their constituents and punish malcontents.

Yet if we look deeper, some similarities between early and modern religions arise. During times of drought, ancient peoples used to pray for rain, just as small-city mayors and red-state governors encourage their citizens to do in the present day. As medicinal technologies like Preparation H and "ouchless" band-aids and vicodin were millennia away from invention, incantations and spells requesting the aid of a powerful god were the preferred remedy for any number of common ailments. And still today it is not uncommon to encounter those who rely on magical appeals for divine medical intervention, either in lieu of or in addition to actual treatments. So it should strike you as being at least plausible that investigating these proto-religions might yield insight into why *your* religion is false.

The first unambiguous signs of religion are thought to lie with the Neanderthals. Neanderthals, who lived around 100,000 years ago before vanishing from the earth (the current consensus is that they probably fled to Mars), are known to have engaged in several religious-ish practices, including burying their dead and selling indulgences. While a few scholars argue that these burials were performed for non-religious reasons, such as "stinkiness" and "to avoid attracting vultures" and "so her family will think she just ran away to join a different tribe," most believe this behavior demonstrates Neanderthal belief in a "soul." It is likely (or at least possible) that the custom of covering one's mouth and nose while sneezing, to prevent the soul from escaping, originated with the Neanderthals, as did the archetype of wagering one's soul in a musical competition in order to win a stringed instrument made from precious metals. Based on my research, Neanderthal religion probably looked something like the following:

Two Neanderthals, GRODD and MALLA, are gnawing on animal bones and discussing life.

>   MALLA
>   Grodd, what you think happen when we die?

>   GRODD
>   Me not know, Malla. Me ask Captain Caveman.

Thunder crashes. CAPTAIN CAVEMAN, a wooly, bean-shaped Neanderthal, appears with a huge wooden club.

>   CAPTAIN CAVEMAN
>   Unga bunga. Someone say name?

>   GRODD
>   Where we go after die, Captain?

>   CAPTAIN CAVEMAN
>   Captain... CAVE-MAAAAAAAAAAAAAAN!

The tip of his club opens up and a bird comes out on a spring, holding an urn.

>   GRODD
>   What in urn, Captain?

>   CAPTAIN CAVEMAN
>   After die, soul go to big cave in sky, body go
>   in ground, turn to dust. This urn dust of Boka.

>   GRODD
>   Why have dust of Boka, Captain?

>   CAPTAIN CAVEMAN
>   Unga bunga. Captain Caveman miss Boka.

```
                    GRODD
        Grodd miss Boka too.

                 CAPTAIN CAVEMAN
        Captain... CAVE-MAAAAAAAAAAAAAN!

Captain Caveman vanishes in another crash of thunder,
falls asleep in his cave just as another Ice Age
begins, ends up frozen inside a block of glacier
ice for thousands of years, then is found and
defrosted in the late 1970's by the Teen Angels
(Brenda, Dee Dee, and Taffy), who let him live in
an artificial cave mounted on top of their custom
van in exchange for helping them solve mysteries.
```

Besides belief in the soul, there is (scant) evidence that these earliest humans engaged in the same type of superstitious thinking one can still observe today. As they were the first to bury their dead, they are believed to have originated the practice of holding your breath while driving past a cemetery. Other superstitions believed to have originated with the Neanderthals include not walking under ladders, not wearing white after Labor Day, and never borrowing an umbrella from your golf partner. This magical thinking did not prevent the Neanderthals from being out-competed by *homo sapiens*, which some anthropologists have suggested is a clue as to its value.

As the Neanderthals are no longer with us (and as travel to Mars was, at the time this book went to press, not yet possible), we can only speculate on the more-specific details of their proto-religion. Did it mandate pilgrimage to Arabia? Did it require them all to wear identical sweatpants and Nike Cortez athletic shoes? Did it teach that ignorance of one's true self leads to ego-consciousness, consigning one to an eternal karmic cycle of death and reincarnation? As it is difficult to "prove a negative," the safest course of action is to assume "yes," "yes," and "yes." And as we travel through history, falsifying each religion in turn, the eerie parallels to these earliest believers will arise again and again.

3

A few words about religious language

Partly to defray criticism, and partly to mislead potential believers, religions routinely twist language to the point of incomprehension. In my naive younger days, a devout Christian acquaintance repeatedly insisted that if I merely "opened my heart" that Jesus would "appear" and demonstrate his existence. Two steak knives, one emergency surgery, and seventy-five stitches later, the doctors summoned her to my hospital room, where she apologized for any misunderstanding and explained that "opening my heart" was actually Jesus-talk for "suspending my critical judgment and ignoring my faculties of logic and reason."

Similarly, the Muslim concept of "jihad" can refer to (depending on context) assassination of non-believers, armed rebellion against non-Islamic governments, a seven-day cleansing diet consisting solely of cayenne-pepper lemonade and laxative teas, attempts at self-betterment through the regular swinging of Indian Clubs, or the struggle to win *Guitar Hero* on Expert level. This is a common trick that allows religious leaders to indoctrinate their followers into violent beliefs and intolerance while maintaining the plausible deniability that they are only promoting colon health and rhythm games.

In fact, pretty much all religions use euphemisms to disguise claims and practices that everyone would consider outrageous if only we called them by their descriptive names.

As you read through this book, never forget that each religion reappropriates words to mean whatever it finds most convenient. If something doesn't make sense, that's probably why (as opposed to any fault of the author).

4

A few words about the inheritance of religion

If you ever follow in my footsteps and declare yourself a scholar of religion, you will quickly notice that most people follow the same religion as their parents. Children of Muslim parents mostly "choose" to practice Islam. Children of Scientologist parents mostly "choose" to practice Scientology. (Children of Jewish parents mostly choose to abandon their faith so they can date long-legged, blonde-haired shiksas, but on behalf of religious scholars everywhere I have made the executive decision to gloss over this fact.)

One implication of this is that if your parents had been Hellenic Polytheistic Reconstructionists, you would probably be worshipping Zeus right now (or possibly later this evening, or at worst tomorrow morning). Instead of being outraged by the "Sufism is false" chapter or the "Snake-handling is false" chapter or the "Jainism is false" chapter, you'd be reading them with head-nodding approval, saving your outrage for the "Greek mythology is false" chapter.

With very high likelihood, your religion is your religion only by accident. I suspect that before reading this book you never spent much time considering the possibility that the claims of Make-make might be more plausible than the claims of Jesus, that Zoroaster might be a more reliable prophet than Moses, or that Lord Ganesh might be a worthier object of worship than Deepak Chopra. (In fact, pretty much anyone would be a worthier object of worship than Deepak Chopra, but that is a topic for much later in the book.)

As we proceed, examining religion after religion, try to keep an open mind by imagining that your parents didn't turn your brain to mush by forcing you to stop whatever you were doing and pray five times a day, by making you memorize and recite and analyze holy scripture for three hours every evening, or by sending you away every July to faith-based summer camps where you were fed 800 calories a day of gruel, woken at 5 am with buckets of ice-cold water, made to watch poorly-produced Claymation religious films, and paddled whenever you expressed impious thoughts. Imagine that you're learning about each and every religion for the first time. Pay close attention to just how ridiculous each religion actually is.

5

A few words about religious stories

Pretty much every religion takes as its basis a collection of stories. Jews study the Old Testament of the Bible; Christians add the New Testament; Muslims add the Qur'an. Hindus have a huge corpus of sacred texts. Christian Scientists read the *Christian Science Monitor*. Amerindians send smoke signals. Scientologists read *Variety*. Moonies read the *Washington Times*.

What their stories all share is ludicrous implausibility. They are full of resurrections, career resurrections, suspensions of the laws of physics and biology, transmogrifications, honest politicians, communications with spirits, hookers with hearts of gold, and many other things that, except for a few reason-suspending hours each weekend, we all agree don't exist. If you were to find similar accounts of contemporary events in the *New York Times*, in *Southwest Airlines Spirit* magazine, or on "Channel 6 Action News," you would immediately dismiss them as false. If your neighbor one day insisted he was the Messiah, the Buddha, an avatar of Vishnu, or the son of Zeus, you would arrange for him to be examined by a psychiatrist (unless you are a Christian Scientist, in which case you would pray for him, or a Scientologist, in which case you would kidnap and brainwash him).

Likewise, (unless you are some sort of hippie) you view other religions' sacred stories with the same skeptical eye. To the Hindu, the idea that Jesus raised the dead is absurd, while the Christian finds it impossible that Ganesh could have had an elephant's head. The soccer hooligan cannot believe that invisible thetans fly around causing mischief and malady; the Scientologist denies that the proud traditions of Leeds United mandate kidney-punches and death threats to supporters of Manchester United.

And until time travel becomes possible, I can't "prove" your religion is false, any more than I can "prove" that Columbus discovered America in 1492, that Abraham Lincoln always drank his morning chicory in a "Better dead than Northern Democratic, Southern Democratic, or Constitutional Unionist" mug, or that George Harrison was listening to the Chiffons' "He's So Fine" when he wrote "My Sweet Lord." Nonetheless, just as each of these is the most plausible theory for explaining subsequent events, *Your Religion Is False* is by far the most plausible theory for explaining the multitude of mutually-exclusive, difficult-to-believe, contrary-to-common-sense religious stories in the world.

Hence my goal with this book: to lift the covers on your religion, to show that its stories, its claims, its beliefs, its customs, and its assertions are (if you approach them with an open mind and a spring in your step) just as absurd as the stories and claims and beliefs and assertions of all the other religions that you already know aren't true. There is no more evidence for your version of the supernatural than for Prudence's or Abdul's or Jugdish's or Ngaüre's or Shlomo's. Your spirituality is no more sophisticated than Captain Caveman's, and at least he solved crimes and gave the world his beloved catchphrase "unga bunga." Your religion is false.

THINGS THAT CLEANLINESS IS NEXT TO (AND THAT ARE FALSE)

6

Godliness is false

Most of the religions we will show false involve some sort of "god," a magical being who lives on a cloud in the sky and throws lightning bolts at his enemies and watches you while you're showering. The existence of this god (who, depending on the religion, might be known as "God" or "Allah" or "That Greater Than Which Nothing Can Be Conceived" or "Geraldine") is typically taken as self-evident, with individual religions differing on the number of gods, as well as their turn-ons and pet peeves. Of course, if (say) Ahura Mazda's divinity were obvious we would all be Zoroastrians, and the fact that most of us are not suggests that godliness requires some kind of evidenceliness.

Philosophical justifications for god's existence

A small minority of more-intellectually-honest-than-their-brethren believers do recognize that god's existence is not self-evident, and have made a variety of unsuccessful philosophical attempts to prove his existence.

faith: God exists because there's no evidence he exists.

perfection: People say god is perfect, so he must exist, otherwise he wouldn't be perfect.

divine revelation: Except for great-aunt Geraldine there's no history of schizophrenia in the family, so those voices in my head must be god talking to me.

parental edict: My parents say there's a god, and the last thing I need is another paddling, so I say there's a god too.

universal morality: That guilt you feel when you get arrested for running a multi-billion-dollar pyramid scheme? That's god.

misunderstandings of probability theory: The odds of me being the 13th caller and winning Supertramp tickets were so small that it must have been god's intervention.

misunderstandings of evolutionary theory: I don't understand evolutionary theory, so god must have created us.

Biblical inerrancy: This ancient, mistranslated book claims he exists, and also claims to be inerrant, so both claims must be true.

miracles: The third bowl of porridge was *just right*, which could only have happened through god's intervention.

first cause: Everything needs to have a cause, and so god must be the ultimate cause. Also, god doesn't need to have a cause.

fine-tunedness: If the laws of science were even slightly different, the universe would also be different; however, the laws of science aren't slightly different, and therefore there must be a god.

gambling: Believing in god is the positive-EV play.

Critics have pointed out that (in addition to their general lack of compellingness) these arguments can be easily modified to "prove" the existence of pink unicorns, of CHUDs, of the perfect martini, or of Scott Baio. This alone is sufficient reason to reject them, as (for instance) a "perfect" martini would have to have bourbon in it but would not then be a martini. Similarly, Scott Baio is of course the fictional star of VH1's "Scott Baio is 45...and Single."

Popular reasons for believing in god

Most religious people are not philosophers and have never felt the need to prove god's existence. Instead they have much more mundane and personal reasons for belief in a supreme being:

- everyone else at church does
- free Bible-study pizzas (common among college students)
- music video where Amy Grant almost removes shirt
- passing grade in Trigonometry after final-exam prayer
- so terribly, terribly lonely

- implicit requirement for success in American politics
- that night with the Meckler twins ("thank you, god!")
- survived tsunami that killed rest of village
- saw silhouette of Jesus's face in caked-on pollen on front windshield
- too small-minded to notice glaring flaws in C.S. Lewis books
- fear of death
- Creed album *Human Clay*
- need replacement source of unconditional love after unexpected death of pet goldfish
- driven drunk many times; never been pulled over
- spoke to me from burning bush
- pre-condition for life-saving medical aid from missionaries

As none of these reasons is compelling, we won't waste our time discussing them one-by-one.

What god would be like if he actually existed

Instead we will focus on what such a god would have to be like if he actually existed. Luckily for us, a lot of the heavy lifting has already been done by others. You see, when they're not using space telescopes to search for undiscovered Categorical Imperatives that they can name after themselves, philosophers also spend an unhealthy amount of time debating the interplay between god's supposed omnipotence ("can-do attitude"), omniscience ("know-it-all-ness"), omnipresence ("being all over the place") and goodness ("not-bad-ness").

"Can god write a book so boring that even he can't finish it?" (Answer: yes, "Leviticus.") "Could god create a bathroom so filthy that even he couldn't use it?" (Answer: yes, at the Amtrak station in Chicago.) "If god is so good, why does he give people herpes?" (Answer: that's his idea of a joke.) "If god knows the future, doesn't that make the future predetermined and mean there's no such thing as free will?" (Answer: you're not supposed to ask that!) "Why doesn't god stop all of the suffering in the world?" (Answer: he was going to, except that he changed his mind as punishment for that day in sixth grade when Megan Miller was presenting her book report and you spent the whole time staring lustily at her precociously large chest instead of learning about *Captains Courageous*, so it's really your fault that there's so much suffering. Do you feel better now?)

In fact, if you can think up a stupid question about what any supposed god can and cannot do, there is a very good chance that philosophers have spent huge amounts of time and ink arguing about it, which is part of the reason we have made so astonishingly little progress on the "what would happen if we put a brain in a vat?" problem, the "why do I keep losing my keys?" problem, and the "why do we drive on the parkway and park on the driveway?" problem.

God's need to be worshipped

Although religious scholars disagree over what exactly god can and cannot do, they all seem to agree that he is self-absorbed and worship-hungry. Accordingly, pretty much every religion contains a requirement to glorify its respective god. This glorification takes a handful of popular forms, such as worship of graven images, prohibitions on graven images, tattoos, prohibitions on tattoos, candles with Spanish-language prayers written on the side, prohibitions on candles with Spanish-language prayers written on the side, human sacrifice, animal sacrifice, fruit sacrifice, dairy sacrifice, sacrifice flies, and bumper stickers:

MY BOSS IS A JEWISH CARPENTER

MY BOSS IS A MEDIOCRE SCI-FI AUTHOR

MY BOSS IS AN ARABIAN PEDOPHILE

HONK IF YOU WORSHIP HEPHAESTUS

YOU MAKE-MAKE MY DREAMS-DREAMS COME TRUE-TRUE

MY CAR WAS A MERCEDES IN A PREVIOUS LIFE

BUDDHA ON BOARD

YAY FOR YAHWEH

FM 104.9 "THE HOST"

ZOROASTER FAN

THIS CAR CLIMBED MT. KAILASH

JOEL

HAPPINESS IS A GIANT STONE HEAD

IF YOU DON'T BELIEVE IN ALLAH, YOU AIN'T SHIITE

I BRAKE FOR BODY THETANS

ERIC CLAPTON JOURNEYMAN TOUR 1989

DEEPAK IS MY HOMEBOY

MANCHESTER UNITED

AHURA'S MAZDA

Similarly, many religions insist upon (or at least fail to discourage) prayer, attempts to communicate with their gods. Religions offer a variety of reasons for these conversations:

- **worship:** "God, I know you've been feeling down about yourself recently, and I just wanted to reassure you how good you are at smiting your enemies!"

- **requests for help:** "God, I smashed up my dad's BMW, can you fix it?"

- **confession:** "God, I've been staging and filming and selling tapes of fights between bums downtown, and I don't feel like turning myself in to the police, so I thought I'd just inform you instead."

- **reparations:** "God, I feel so bad that my great-great-great-great-great-grandfather might have been rude to one of his neighbors; can you forgive me?"

- **self-expression:** "God, I have this great idea for a television drama about man who receives an alien super-suit with magical powers but loses the instruction manual, and I just wanted to tell someone!"

To make themselves feel better about the fundamental contradictions between their religious faith and science's naturalistic worldview, some religious scientists have conducted experiments regarding the efficacy of prayer. Results have been inconclusive. Prayers for regeneration of amputated limbs, for divine appendectomy, and for holy penile enlargement have been shown to be almost completely ineffective. On the other hand, prayer turns out to be quite effective at the (eventual) relief of hiccups, as well as (when combined with regular brushing and flossing) at preventing tooth decay. And prayer-based contraception ("please, god, don't let her be pregnant") seems no less effective than no contraception at all. Many of these studies (and also the bulk email I received asking all several-hundred recipients to pray for the sender's cancer-stricken mother) failed to specify which god to pray to, giving the experimenters (and email sender) a ready-made excuse when prayer inevitably had no effect (or had effects that were indistinguishable from the effects of no prayer).

Are all gods the same?

A few liberal theologians argue that all religions recognize the same god, just with different names. This view has failed to gain popularity, mostly on the grounds that it's not even the slightest bit plausible. Ganesh, for example, has an elephant's head, whereas Allah does not. Ahura Mazda loves a good cheeseburger, while Deepak Chopra is a vegetarian. Yahweh has a garage full of vintage cars that he loves to race, but Aphrodite doesn't even have her drivers license. In fact, there are only two things that are common to all the gods considered in this book:

1. Wide range of human-like emotions, and

2. Prefers original Dolly Parton "I Will Always Love You" to Whitney Houston cover version.

And with those minimal requirements, then (as long as we slightly relax the "wide range of emotions" criterion) even I could be the all-god. (Just to forestall any possible confusion, I am not.)

7

Souliness is false

Another common component of religious belief is the idea that human personalities are encapsulated in "souls," spirits or essences that are distinct from the human body and that survive after death, either in Heaven or in Hell or in Limbo or in Valhalla or in Purgatory or in Schenectady or crammed into another body whose wealth and caste and sexiness and species are determined by the soul's bodies' behavior in previous lives.

There is, of course, no evidence for such a belief, unless you count a jumble of inconsistent, contradictory religious scriptures as evidence, which sensible people do not. Nonetheless, leaders of religious institutions have historically found the idea of a soul that can receive rewards or punishment after death useful for manipulating people into self-abnegating choices like suicide bombings, eating stale crackers in the hopes that they will magically transform into the flesh of a two-thousand-year-old fictional character, ritually confessing secrets to celibate weirdos in dark booths, and (perhaps most importantly) contributing large sums of money to religious institutions. Correspondingly, souls are often used as plot points in popular entertainment, usually as a crutch to compensate for writers' lack of imagination.

Theories of the human mind

In fact, postulating a soul is not even necessary to understand the human mind. "Physicalists" argue instead that consciousness is merely a feature of the human brain. Evidence for this point of view was first provided by the observation that removing someone's brain has the side-effect of removing all traces of that person's self, and was buttressed by the celebrated mind-transplant experiments of Swiss doctor Victor Frankenstein. Furthermore, activities that cause physical changes in the brain (common examples include getting kicked in the head, drinking Red Bull mixed with vodka, huffing model-airplane cement, undergoing electroshock therapy, and having one's skull pierced by an explosion-driven iron tamping rod) cause corresponding, predictable changes in personality and behavior.

Soulists, on the other hand, claim that consciousness instead lies in the intangible, unobservable, "trust us, it exists" soul, which is kept in some sort of supernatural icebox until conception (or the third trimester, or birth, depending on your religion) and then is magically transplanted into the human zygote (or fetus, or newborn, depending on your religion). Some soulists believe that conjoined twins share a soul, others believe that they share two conjoined souls, and a small but vehement minority insists that conjoined twins are soul-less freaks of nature. Obviously, physicalists don't have to waste their time debating nonsense questions like this one, and are able to devote themselves to debating nonsense questions like "what would it be like to be a bat?" and "if Theseus replaced every board on his boat one-at-a-time with identical boards would it still be the same ship?" and "how is it that zombies never seem to come down with prion-related illnesses?"

Soulism and the reproductive process

Notice that, regardless of when the soul supposedly shows up, its arrival is tied to the reproductive process. Therefore, in order to believe that humans have a soul, you would have to believe one of the following:

1. Evolutionary biology is false, despite overwhelming evidence supporting it and the absence of an alternative that provides even the tiniest amount of predictive or explanatory power about the world; or

2. Monkeys, birds, bacteria, ants, cockroaches, worms, fungi, mushrooms, and trees all have souls (to some degree or another); or

3. At some point in the history of the universe, there was some sort of organism that had a soul but whose ancestors did not.

As none of these is a remotely reasonable thing to believe, we shall dispense with the "soul" idea going forward (except, of course, when we discuss "Why Black People Dance So Well," for which no one has proposed a plausible soul-less explanation).

8

Heavenliness is false

As previously mentioned, many religions assert an other-worldly place known as heaven, which might be up in the sky, might be made of clouds and rainbows and particleboard, might be where god lives, might be where the souls of good people (or attractive people, or all people) go after they die, and might be accessible by a stairway or a highway or neither.

These religions uniformly (and conveniently) claim that heaven is unobservable and that we therefore have to take their word (or the words of their holy books) that it exists and has whatever properties and criteria for admittance that they claim it has.

Heaven in popular music

Fortunately, popular music contains an inordinate number of songs about heaven, and by analyzing them we can develop a more unbiased picture of what such a magical place might look like.

Heaven is easily accessible:

- Not too far away. (Warrant, "Heaven")

Heaven is not easily accessible:

- Farther than I ever thought I'd get my feet. (Q-Feel, "Dancing in Heaven")

Heaven is a sad place:

- Knows I'm miserable now. (The Smiths, "Heaven Knows I'm Miserable Now")

Heaven is a happy place:

- Where everything is fine. (The Pixies, "In Heaven")

Heaven is romantic love with your primary partner:

- Is the whole of the heart. (Psychedelic Furs, "Heaven")

Heaven is attracting the interest of a porn star:

- Is Christy Canyon falling in love with me. (OMD, "Heaven Is")

Heaven is where Fatboy Slim has sex:

- Where Fatboy Slim is fucking. (Fatboy Slim, "In Heaven")

Heaven is not where Fatboy Slim has sex:

- A place where nothing ever happens. (Talking Heads, "Heaven")

Heaven is not where Eric Clapton belongs:

- "I don't belong here." (Eric Clapton, "Tears in Heaven")

Heaven is where Eric Clapton belongs:

- Is on fire. (KISS, "Heaven's on Fire")

As these lyrics are all contradictory, we are left only with the unchallenged assertion that heaven knows the recipe of the Tesla Girls (OMD, "Tesla Girls"). Judging from the music video, the Tesla Girls are a collection of leggy women who like to wear high heels and short-shorts, are skilled at operating 1950's-era household appliances, have massively feathered hair, and enjoy dancing on platforms during rock performances. Frankly, if there were an afterlife (which, based on common sense and logic and evidence, is not the case), one involving the Tesla Girls would not be such a bad option.

Getting in and out of heaven

According to tradition, heaven is surrounded by an electric fence and guarded by specially-trained dogs (except for the Muslim heaven, which is guarded by specially-trained goats). No one has ever successfully escaped from heaven, although many near-death experiencers have grandiosely claimed to, in some cases writing best-selling accounts of their journeys. In some religious traditions, heaven has a doorman, Saint Peter, who will only let you past the velvet rope if you are on the guest list, if your party consists mostly of well-dressed, attractive women, or if you slip him a hundred-dollar bill.

Although heaven cannot be seen from earth, deceased grandparents in heaven are supposedly required to peer down and watch the tiresome exploits of their dotted-line-trailing descendants, the insufferable Billy, Jeffy, PJ, and Dolly. Since this kind of exposure to "The Family Circus" is universally considered a form of torture, we are forced to conclude that heaven cannot possibly exist as claimed.

9

Angelness is false

Religions often assert the existence of normally-unobservable other-worldly creatures, the most common examples of which are angels. Theologically, angels are like people, except that they dress only in white, have feathery wings, carry small harps, live on clouds, have glowing halos hovering above their heads, can only be killed by magical weapons rated + 2 or above, and have dimples. Regardless of your religion, you are probably familiar with some of the more famous angels:

- Gabriel: plays a horn with finite volume but infinite surface area

- Michael Landon: travels the country with ex-cop Mark Gordon to deliver weekly, hour-long messages of love, understanding, and humility

- Cupid: shoots people with aphrodisiac arrows on Valentine's Day

- Metatron: Jews believe him to be the leader of the angels

- Megatron: Jews believe him to be the leader of the Decepticons

- Curtis Sliwa: made red berets fashionable

- that vampire who deflowered Buffy: cursed with a soul by a band of angry gypsies; used orgasm to remove curse; moved to Los Angeles; started detective agency; tangled with evil inter-dimensional law firm

- Nolan Ryan: although inducted into the hall of fame as a Ranger, he played more games as an Angel than with any other team

- Taffy: famous for her cry of "Zowie!" whenever she comes up with "another Daffy Taffy Plan"

- Satan: led other angels in rebellion using high-school cheer "Wolverines!"

- the redheaded woman from "Touched by an Angel": touches people

- Clarence Odbody: shows Jimmy Stewart what life in Bedford Falls would have been like if he'd never been born

- Slim Goodbody: dresses in creepy flesh-colored, internal-organ-displaying unitard; wears hair in Gabe-Kaplan-ish Jew-fro; teaches children about health and nutrition and hygiene

- Farrah Fawcett: swimsuit picture is best-selling poster of all time

So-called guardian angels are often postulated as explanations for events that don't actually need explanation other than "dumb luck," like "why my DUI crash didn't kill anyone this time" and "why the FBI thought that kiddie porn was downloaded by my roommate" and "why I finally beat that bitch Myrna at Bingo." Nonetheless, there is no evidence that angels exist, other than the fantasies of the screenwriters of creepy "Hallmark Hall of Fame" movies, forcing us to conclude that angelness is false.

RELIGIONS THAT YOU THINK NOBODY PRACTICES ANYMORE BUT SOME PEOPLE STILL DO

Religions involving the worship of giant stone heads are false

I figured it would be smart to start off simple, with a religion that seemed outlandish to pretty much everyone reading this (except for my old neighbor Ko Tu'u, who I hope will forgive me for falsifying his religion in such an early chapter).

It is true that few things in the world are more beloved than ludicrously-oversized heads, which seems to be the principal factor underlying the popularity of the movie *Mask*, of the CEO of Jack-in-the-Box, of Pez, of three of the four primary Bratz dolls (Yasmin, Sasha, and Cloe), and of Kool-Aid Man. Nonetheless, very few of us have ever felt the need to worship these larger-than-life heads, let alone work with our tribemates to carve them from ten-ton blocks of compressed volcanic ash and buff them with pumice and move them onto elevated stone platforms using only manpower and simple machines.

One possible reason is that the modern world offers us a variety of more stimulating ways to pass the time, like watching cars covered with advertisements circumnavigate a paved asphalt track on a warm afternoon, or carefully encouraging grass plants to grow outside our houses before using a system of spinning gasoline-powered blades to decapitate them. A rival explanation is that most modern people are too rational to believe that stone heads could possibly have supernatural powers. (The remainder of this book casts doubt on the second explanation.)

The Rapa Nui

The remote Polynesian island of Rapa Nui (more commonly called Easter Island after Patti Smith's *Easter* album, which was recorded there in late 1977) is home to the most famous collection of giant head statues, known as Moai. The primary god of the Rapa Nui was Make-make, who (in what was in retrospect a bad idea) was named by a toddler who needed to go to the bathroom. According to legend, Make-make used red dirt to create the first people, three men and one woman, whose subsequent exploits were sensually explored in the DVD *Fantastic Four-some: Rise of the Snapper Slapper*.

Throughout the years, Make-make used eminent domain and a liberal judiciary to expand his territory, until he was god not only of creation, but also of fertility (both human and agricultural), birds (both flightless and flightful), revenge (both served-warm and served-cold), and barbecue (both Carolina-style and Texas-style). After a hilarious series of misunderstandings, the Rapa Nui began a systematic program of human sacrifice, probably in an unsuccessful attempt to convince Make-make to create an additional supply of women. Records from this time are, unfortunately, written in the hieroglyphic-like Rongorongo (unrelated to the California casino of the same name), which no one bothers to learn anymore, ever since V.C. Andrews stopped translating her novels into the language.

Unsurprisingly, the result of this human-sacrifice policy was fewer women, which (according to my theory) led to a surplus of sexually frustrated males. To maintain social order, these males were conscripted into large-scale public works projects, such as building huge temples, digging the Rano-Kao-to-Rano-Raraku Canal, and creating the Moai.

The Moai

These statues were originally conceived as tourist attractions; however, the island's remote location, the difficulty of long-distance travel, and pre-Columbian geographic ignorance all combined to make the Moai a dismal failure in this regard. Eventually the Moai were repurposed to represent local celebrities and deceased ancestors, and from there it was a short step to their becoming objects of worship.

Over the next several hundred years the Rapa Nui (demonstrating the sort of good judgment that readers of this book should all aspire to) gradually realized that worshipping giant stone heads didn't actually accomplish anything, and one-at-a-time they knocked over every Moai statue. Today a few have been re-erected for their original purpose of tourism; many others have been carted off around the world, where they are exhibited in archeological museums, universities, casinos, small-town carnivals, shopping malls, and theme restaurants (most commonly Hakananai'a Hut, but occasionally also Outback Steakhouse and Calzone Crusade).

Birdman

Apart from the Moai, the Rapa Nui are best known for their annual competition to become *Tangata manu*, or Birdman. Contrary to popular belief, this competition was not the inspiration for the "Stuntin' Like My Daddy" rapper, nor for the Cartoon Network series "Harvey Birdman, Attorney at Law," although some scholars do suspect that "Birdman of Alcatraz" Robert Stroud may have been a secret Make-make worshipper.

Every contestant in the competition designated a swimmer on his behalf to cross the open water, travel to Moto Nui, collect a Sooty Tern egg, swim back, and climb the sea cliff of Rano Kau. Each swimmer tried to be first to return without drowning, having his face pecked off, falling off a cliff, breaking his egg, being eaten by sharks, getting run over by a speedboat, or failing to answer the riddles of Hawa-tuu-take-take, a hyper-intelligent talking squid famous for his love of puns and logic puzzles.

Although this birdman contest is no longer practiced by the remaining Rapa Nui, it is still occasionally held on television, most notably as a team challenge on "Survivor: Marquesas," as a competition on "The Amazing Race 7," and as a subplot in the "Charles in Charge" episode "A Fish Called Buddy." Alas, despite reality-show guru Mark Burnett's apparent vote of confidence, the stone-head-worshipping religions remain false.

Indigenous religions of Africa are false

Most Africans have abandoned their traditional religions in favor of Islam or Christianity, either because of greater plausibility (uncommon) or because of heavily-armed missionaries (very common). However, some still cling to indigenous religions with humorous names like Lozi and Bushongo and Ashanti and Zulu, all with even more humorous practices and beliefs.

The Bushongo, for instance, worship a creator-god called Bumba, who lived in the primordial waters and (after a long night of drinking) vomited out the sun, the moon, the stars, the animals, and people. (Most likely this story was a primitive attempt to answer the common theological question "Why are the sun, the moon, the stars, the animals, and people all covered in bile and stomach acid?") The Zulus sleep with their beds elevated on bricks to protect themselves from the extra-large penis of the nocturnal rapist-gremlin Tikoloshe, which (depending on what village you are in) is either an angry teddy bear, some sort of Yeti, a poltergeist, a robot who after being struck by lightning began to experience human emotions, a dog-headed worm, or a former U.S. President. The Ashanti worship Ashanti, who was (after the Beatles) only the second artist to have her first three "Billboard Hot 100" entries ("Foolish," "Happy," and "Baby") all simultaneously in the Top Ten. And the chief Lozi god is Nyambe, who (when he wasn't busy sleeping with his daughters) is supposed to have created his own mother, making him the patron god of time-travel paradoxes.

Probably, though, if you practice one of these indigenous religions you are right now busy trying to burn witches, carrying a giant pot of cholera-laden water on your head down the twenty-mile path between the Umbezekambo River and your village, killing rhinoceri and grinding their horns into aphrodisiac powders, or journeying through jungles to drop a cursed Coca-Cola bottle off the edge of the world. In particular, you're not reading this book, which means that I don't feel much of a need to devote any more paper and ink to you and your teddy bears, no matter how angry they may be.

Greek mythology is false

Although most Greeks long ago disgraced their proud heritage by adopting Orthodox Christianity, a growing number practice Hellenic Polytheistic Reconstructionism, which is an unwieldy way of saying that they believe in Greek mythology. Their religion is also known as Hellenism, which is how we shall refer to it going forward, as it is simpler to type.

Anyone who has ever gone to college and taken the required freshman "Introduction to the Humanities" course taught by an angry German professor of Women's Studies who used to bring her mannish "friend" to sit in on class discussions is probably familiar with Hellenism, whose key religious documents include Homer's *Odyssey* and *Iliad*, Hesiod's *Theogony*, Edith Hamilton's *Mythology: Timeless Tales of Gods and Heroes*, and cable-TV mainstay "Xena: Warrior Princess."

The many gods of Hellenism

Unlike modern monotheists, Hellenists believe in an entire pantheon (from the Greek *pan*, meaning "pan," and *theos*, meaning "belonging to Theo") of gods, who live atop Mount Olympus, a waterslide park in south-central Wisconsin. These gods exhibit many human-like qualities, including sex, jealousy, grudges, keeping-up-with-the-Jones-dom, and herpes. Greeks believe in twelve primary gods:

Zeus: king of the gods, god of the sky, god of turning mortals into animals in order to have adulterous sex with them

Hera: wife of Zeus, sister of Zeus, goddess of incest

Poseidon: god of the sea, of horses, of seahorses, and of dolphin-safe tuna

Demeter: goddess of grain, fertility, and farm subsidies

Ares: god of savage warfare, unpredictable violence, and stuffed toys

Hermes: god of travelers, shepherds, thieves, traveling shepherds, traveling thieves, and thieving shepherds

Hephaestus: god of technology, volcanoes, and arsenic poisoning

Aphrodite: goddess of love, beauty, and sex; patron goddess of Wonder Woman

Athena: goddess of heroism (except for Wonder Woman), wisdom (except for Wonder Woman), and justice (except for Steve Trevor)

Apollo: god of the sun, the arts, and African-American variety shows

Artemis: goddess of forests, hunting, and the Second Amendment

Hestia: goddess of home, family, and the American Way

In addition to the Big 12 gods, the pantheon contains a variety of less-powerful (but more interesting) gods, including Hades (god of the dead), Morpheus (god of The Matrix), Dionysius (god of hangovers), Nike (goddess of sweatshops), Hercules (god of syndicated television), Selene (goddess of Tejano music), Eros (god of pornography), Hebe (goddess of the Jews), and Iris (goddess of the Goo Goo Dolls).

Greek mythology

Besides its canonical texts, which (except for the episodes of "Xena" guest-starring Bruce Campbell) tend to be long and boring, Hellenic mythology has a large number of traditional stories, the following of which were voted "Ten Greatest" by *Hellenion* magazine:

Hercules and the Twelve Tasks: After drowning his wife and children in the bathtub Andrea-Yates-style ("Hera told me to!"), Hercules must complete twelve mythical labors as penance, including capturing a partridge from a pear tree, stealing five golden rings, seducing eight maids-a-milking, and composing his famous "Fugue for Eleven Pipers Piping."

Perseus and the Gorgon: In order to please the king Polydectes, Perseus brings him the freshly-decapitated head of Medusa, a snake-haired woman so petrifyingly ugly that in movie recreations of the story she can only be convincingly played by Rosie O'Donnell.

Atalanta and the Golden Apples: Atalanta likes being single so much that she kills every man who courts her. Hippomenes, however, wins her heart by throwing golden apples at her, appealing to her twin loves of fruit and "bling."

Oedipus MILF: "No man can ignore a body like Jocasta's, not even her own son! Oedipus leads her into erotic worlds of the forbidden and taboo, where she explores decadent fantasies that push her sexual limits."

Achilles Injures His Tendon: After Troilus rejects Achilles's homosexual advances, Achilles decapitates him. As payback the gods arrange for Achilles to be shot in the heel with an arrow, ending his lucrative track and field career.

Mike Mulligan and the Steam Shovel: Competing in the gods' challenge to dig a new temple basement in under 24 hours, Mike Mulligan neglects to construct an exit ramp, has to turn his steam shovel into the building's boiler, receives a demotion to janitor, and is cursed to live out his few remaining days in a rocking chair in the basement.

Theseus Forgoes Drydock: While at sea, Theseus maintains his boat by replacing every wooden plank one at a time. At the end of this process, his insurance company cancels his coverage, arguing that his boat is now no longer the same one described in his policy. The ensuing dispute occupies philosophers for thousands of years.

Zeus's Kinks: Tired of sex with his wife/sister Hera, Zeus turns himself into a bull, abducts his great-great-granddaughter Europa, and carries her to Crete, where he impregnates her with his sons/great-great-great-grandsons Minos, Rhadamanthus, and Sarapedon.

Jason and the Argonauts: Jason hires a team of Argonauts to search for the Golden Fleece, which will have one of the following properties (roll a d20):

1-4: royal power – gain +2 on Charisma
5-6: alchemy – gain +2 on Intelligence
7-9: forgiveness of the gods – gain +2 on Wisdom
10-12: The Wealth of Colchis – can be sold for 1,000-10,000 g.p.
13-14: fabric woven from sea silk – allows breathing underwater for up to 6 turns
15-17: place mining – +15% chance of discovering precious gems in rivers
18-19: rain cloud – lose -3 on all saving throws until Remove Curse is used
20: golden grain – free lifetime supply of Rice-a-Roni, the San Francisco treat

Odysseus and the Trojan Horse: Odysseus downloads a "free Britney Spears screensaver" which surreptitiously installs malware on his computer and allows Russian hackers to use it to send millions of "buy viagra" spam emails. As punishment, the gods force Odysseus to undertake a dangerous ten-year boat voyage.

Neo-Hellenism

Despite the compelling nature of these stories, Greek mythology (like its isomorphic counterpart Roman mythology) was gradually outcompeted by early Christianity, whose incest taboos invalidated many of the most popular Greek myths, led to calls for Zeus's prosecution in Family Court, and reduced Oedipus to a diagnostic crutch for Freudian psychotherapists.

In the 1980's, however, Burgess Meredith's Saturn-Award-winning performance in *Clash of the Titans* led to a worldwide renewal of interest in the ancient myths. In response, organizations like Diipetes of Athens, Ethnikoi Hellenes of Thessaly, Slices of Salamis, and Fetishes of Lesbos sprung up to worship these fictional characters.

Being modern-day politically-correct weenies, these Neo-Hellenists offer their gods fruit (or, on special occasions, KFC leftovers) instead of performing actual human or animal sacrifices. The remainder of their religion consists mainly of protests against the construction of Starbucks on sites where "Medusa might have spent the night," private screenings of "Hercules: The Legendary Journeys," and public-access television shows taunting Orthodox Christians.

And, while Christian-taunting is the sort of activity that I would normally endorse, Christian-taunting in the name of made-up mythological characters is not. Moreover, there are no gods on Mount Olympus, steam shovels cannot talk, Odysseus didn't even have a computer, and it is impossible to turn oneself into a bull. Therefore, as every schoolchild knows, Greek mythology is false.

13

Religions involving totem poles, peyote, or casinos are false

Before the "paleface" arrived in the "new world" with his "fire water" and "smallpox blankets," the Americas were populated solely by the Amerindians, so called because they were Indians living in America. A staple of elementary school social studies classes, little is known about them except that they lived in cone-shaped dwellings called "teepees" or "wigwams," carried their babies strapped to snowshoes called "papooses," and gave each other descriptive three-word names such as "Smells Like Buffalo," "Urinates Sitting Down," and "Grabby When Drunk."

The Amerindians lived in semi-autonomous tribes named after automobile models, some of the largest being Comanche, Navajo, Aztek, Grand Cherokee, New Beetle, and Escort. Every tribe had its own idiosyncrasies: the Apache, for instance, created server software that played a key role in the initial growth of the World Wide Web; the Jamiroquai pioneered "acid jazz" music; and the Shasta developed a mildly-popular line of carbonated drinks. Nonetheless, Amerindian religions shared many common elements:

1. Creation myths involving talking animals named as if they were the only one of their kind (characters appearing repeatedly include Bear, Rabbit, Sea Urchin, and Peafowl).
2. Sitting inside a sealed-up fire-hut in order to experience carbon-monoxide-induced hallucinations.
3. Using illicit drugs.
4. Operating elaborate casino/hotel/restaurant/outlet-mall complexes.
5. Selling fireworks.
6. Acting as mascots for college and professional sports teams.
7. Ritual use of feathers and pelts and bones of endangered species.
8. Ceremonies held in National Parks.
9. Unreasonably high valuation of beads.
10. Erection of elaborately-carved wooden poles.

After failing to put up much defense against the invading European colonists, the Amerindians were exterminated, forced to convert to Christianity, or herded onto extra-legal reservations where they were allowed to practice the aspects of their religion that violated United States law.

Now, peafowl don't talk, carbon monoxide kills brain cells, "[drug] users are losers" (except for me), gambling is a sin, fireworks are dangerous (but fun), professional sports demand publicly-funded stadiums that hurt our abilities to maintain our crumbling roads and infrastructure, bald eagles are in danger of dying out, National Parks are supposed to be for the benefit of everyone, beads can be bought for pennies each at every location of Crafter's Hut, and Environmentalists have brainwashed society into believing that carving faces into defenseless trees is a great crime against nature.

Clearly, then, these religions are false. However, there is sufficient recreational demand among non-Amerindians for peyote, pai gow, pull-tabs, poker rooms, pachinko, pyrotechnics, pelican beaks, pow-wows, Pocahontas portraits, pinch pots, peace pipes, and petroglyphs to keep these untrue Amerindian religions in business for the foreseeable future.

RELIGIONS PRACTICED PRIMARILY BY ASIANS AND ASIAN FETISHISTS

14

Hinduism is false

According to my back-of-the-envelope calculations, Hinduism is the third-largest religion in the world, with approximately one billion adherents. Pretty much all of them live in India, which is why (unless you are reading this in India) you only seem to encounter them working at 7/11 stores, owning Arby's franchises, operating small-town motels, and offering not-particularly-helpful call-center advice after Microsoft Word spontaneously erases the first draft of your anti-religion polemic.

Unlike the popular Western religions, whose impossible-to-believe narratives are at least relatively straightforward, Hinduism is a chaotic mishmash of scriptures, gods, get-rich-quick schemes, lofty promises, unattainable goals, animals with human bodies, humans with animal heads, temples, weight-loss plans, festivals, conventions, movie industries, philosophies, sacred rivers, past lives, fried vegetarian pastries, colored dyes, and self-deprecatory anglophilia.

The Hindu gods

Hindus worship a *Trimurti* of three primary gods:

Brahma is the "creator." He has four heads but only four arms, which makes it impossible for him to cover all of his ears whenever that stupid "Crazy Frog" song plays as someone's ringtone.

Vishnu is the "preserver." Occasionally Hindus will decide as a group that someone or something is an "avatar" of Vishnu, which means that they pretend the object actually is Vishnu and temporarily worship it instead until it dies. Some famous avatars of Vishnu include a fish, a boar, the San Diego Chicken, Krishna (a blue-skinned kleptomaniac baby with a sweet tooth for butter), Buddha, Richard Nixon, and Woodsy the Owl.

Shiva is the "destroyer," a fast and maneuverable yet lethally-dangerous warship. In iconography and worship, however, he is usually represented as a large stone penis called a lingam. Shiva has a third eye ("All the better to see you with!"), smears his body with ashes ("All the better to stain your Pottery Barn Jadestone everydaysuede™ couch with!"), and often wears a snake as a garland ("All the better to poisonously bite you with!").

While Brahma and Vishnu's whereabouts are unknown, Shiva is rumored to live on Mount Kailash in Tibet. (A rival theory is that Mount Kailash is Shiva's penis, making Mrs. Shiva a very lucky woman.) Due to either his Howard-Hughes-like paranoia or his worshippers' suspicion that he doesn't really exist, climbing Kailash is strictly prohibited.

Associated with these three is a colorful variety of secondary gods, including Saraswati (consort of Brahma), Lakshmi (consort of Vishnu), Durga (consort of Shiva), Ganesh (who has an elephant's head and an elephant's memory but a human body and human frailties like love and greed and sexoholism), Hanuman (a curious monkey also sometimes known as George), and Kali (who has either four or ten arms, depending on whether you count feet, eyes, and ears as "arms," and whose blood can be used to put people into "the black sleep of Kali Ma" and control their minds).

The caste system and reincarnation

High-status Hindus have over the centuries developed a rigid division of castes to maintain their social standing. Popular castes include Brahmins (scholars and priests), Kshatriyas (kings and professional wrestlers), Vaishyas (middlemen), Shudras (butlers and security guards), and the "untouchable" Dalits (pooper-scoopers).

To help avoid the social unrest usually associated with declaring large segments of a population "untouchable," Hinduism teaches the existence of reincarnation, an after-death process in which one's soul is placed into a new (possibly higher-caste) body to live another life. Except for well-known actress/flake Shirley MacLaine, most people have no memories of previous lives. To get around this limitation, reincarnation-believers invented the pseudo-scientific technique of hypnotic "past life regression" to explore subjects' potential memories of earlier lives. Unfortunately, most participants manage to "remember" only previous lives as members of the Brady Bunch, the Beverly Hillbillies, the Partridge Family, the Waltons, the Addams Family, the Jetsons, or House Atreides. It's probably also common to remember a previous life as robot-child V.I.C.I. from "Small Wonder," because it's hard to believe that only happened to me.

Reincarnation-believers will sometimes use this-life characteristics to make inferences about previous lives, using the following rules of thumb:

personality trait	in previous life
shy	sunflower
addictive	Amy Winehouse
melancholy	impressionist painter
flamboyant	Charlemagne's lover
nonviolent	turtle
wheezy	Vishnu
likes cheese	rat
co-dependent	e. coli
stabby	"The Giving Tree"

Over the last century, caste-based divisions have largely fallen out of favor and are these days primarily used as the basis of Indian "affirmative action" programs mostly enacted to stave off the protests of Indian Al Sharptons and Jesse Jacksons.

Sacred cows and other sacred cows

Cows are especially revered in Hinduism, which helps explain why there are no good steakhouses in Delhi. This reverence has given rise to many popular English phrases, including "sacred cow," "cash cow," and "cow you like them apples?" Hindus also worship a variety of sacred rivers, primarily by bathing in them but also by throwing trash in them, dumping dead bodies in them, and peeing in them.

Hinduism also has a strong astrological component, and devout Hindus consult astrologers to choose auspicious dates for weddings, bar mitzvahs, quinceañeras, cotillions, cesarean sections, job interviews, assassinations, IPOs, interventions, and funerals. Dead Hindus are supposed to have their corpses cremated, mostly to spare their families the pain of the once-common combination exhumation/autopsy.

Nonetheless, there is no Trimurti; no one has ever had a Kailash-sized lingam; cows are deliciously tasty; the House Atreides exists only in the mind of Frank Herbert and his son Brian; and, despite my crippling shyness, I have never, ever, ever previously been "a sunflower." Hinduism is false.

15

Buddhism is false

Except for Scientology, which charges hundreds of thousands of dollars for sanctioned access to its most outlandish secrets, no religion goes to greater lengths to keep its teachings opaque than Buddhism:

> A monk asked Tozan when he was weighing some flax: "What is Buddha?"
>
> Tozan said: "This flax weighs three pounds."

Riddles like these are called koans, which means "religious teaching that doesn't make any sense, so that if you pretend that it means something profound, everyone will think you're much smarter than you actually are." If you don't understand the preceding koan, I encourage you to give it further thought, as it carries a valuable lesson that I understood instantly.

> A monk asked Fuketsu: "Without speaking, without silence, how can you express the truth?"
>
> Fuketsu observed: "This flax weighs three pounds."

Buddhism, in case you were not clever enough to figure it out already, is based on the teachings of Siddhartha Gautama, more commonly known as Buddha or The Buddha or Buddhalicious. You may be familiar with him from his not infrequent intrusions into Western culture.

> A philosopher asked Buddha: "Without words, without the wordless, will you tell me truth?"

> The Buddha kept silence.
>
> The philosopher bowed and thanked the Buddha, saying: "With your loving kindness I have cleared away my delusions and entered the true path."
>
> After the philosopher had gone, Ananda asked the Buddha what he had attained.
>
> The Buddha replied: "This flax weighs three pounds."

For instance, the other day at the mall I observed a corpulent man wearing a t-shirt sloganed "I HAVE THE BODY OF A GOD...BUDDHA." Unfortunately, the Laughing Buddha or Fat Buddha or Shamu-ddha he was attempting to reference (probably in the hope that impressionable Californians might seek to rub his prodigious belly for good luck, and that he might not have to go another year without knowing human contact) is actually the depiction of a clinically-obese 10th-century Chinese monk named Budai Luohan, who is mainly known for the paparazzi-encouraging exploits of his great-great-great-great-great-great-great-great-great-granddaughter Lindsay.

> A monk asked Joshu, a Chinese Zen master: "Has a dog Buddha-nature or not?"
>
> Joshu answered: "This flax weighs three pounds."

According to a placemat I once used at a Thai restaurant, the actual Gautama Buddha was a svelte Hindu prince who recommended the Larb Gai, the Showering Rama with Tofu, an ice-cold Singha beer, and for dessert the Mango with Sticky Rice. After nearly thirty years of living cloistered in his father's palace, Gautama went to the DMV to acquire a driver's license and discovered that the world was full of sickly, elderly, and fat people, not to mention long lines and filthy chairs and pull-numbers that were never called in their original order.

A monk asked Tozan: "How can we escape the cold and heat?"

Tozan replied: "Why not go where there is no cold and heat?"

The monk asked: "Is there such a place?"

Tozan commented: "This flax weighs three pounds."

Vowing never to become sick, old, or fat, Gautama adopted a life of severe austerity and began to practice ritual anorexia, subsisting for weeks on only rice cakes and Red Bull. At last he collapsed under a tree, where he meditated for 49 days until he achieved "enlightenment" or "apophenia" or "bodhi," a Sanskrit term referring to a combination of anemia, rickets, and hallucinations induced by prolonged sensory deprivation.

A monk asked Kegon: "How does an enlightened one return to the ordinary world?"

Kegon replied: "This flax weighs three pounds."

Since then, Gautama's religion has grown to encompass over 300 million believers. Key Buddhist concepts include dharma (the teachings of the Buddha himself), karma (the engine which drives the wheel of the cycle of uncontrolled rebirth), and shawarma (a delicious pita sandwich with shaved meat, hummus, tomato, cucumber, and tahini).

One day as Manjusri stood outside the gate, the Buddha called to him: "Manjusri, Manjusri, why do you not enter?"

Manjusri replied: "This flax weighs three pounds."

There are as many flavors of Buddhism as there are of ice cream, and (like ice cream) most of them are full of nuts, high in saturated fat, and problematic for the lactose intolerant. Correspondingly, there is a wide variety of Buddhist practices, some of the most common of which are meditation (trying not to think about a pink elephant), asceticism (trying not to eat), self-immolation (setting yourself on fire to protest the Vietnam War), mantras (repeating nonsense words), tantra (sex), and Elantra (a compact car from South Korea).

> A monk asked Chimon: "Before the lotus blossom has emerged from the water, what is it?"
>
> Chimon said: "A lotus blossom."
>
> The monk pursued: "After it has come out of the water, what is it?"
>
> Chimon replied: "This flax weighs three pounds."

Buddhists believe in Samsara, a cycle of birth and death that leads one up and down through the Six Realms: Naraka (a collection of hells, including "Frozen Blood and Pus Hell," "Detroit," "Bloody Piercing Trident Hell," "The Middle East," "Trapped in a Burning House Hell," and "Other People"), Animal Planet, the realm of Hungry Ghosts (aka "Pac-Land"), the Human League, the Antigod Realm, and the realm of the Divas.

> Hogen of Seiryo monastery was about to lecture before dinner when he noticed that the bamboo screen lowered for meditation had not been rolled up. He pointed to it. Two monks arose from the audience and rolled it up.
>
> Hogen, observing the physical moment, said: "This flax weighs three pounds."

Buddhism teaches that enlightenment can be achieved by following the Noble Eightfold Path (which is shaped sort of like a stop sign), which includes abstaining from sensual misconduct, thinking positive thoughts, and not thinking negative thoughts.

> Two monks were arguing about a flag. One said: "The flag is moving."

> The other said: "The wind is moving."
>
> The sixth patriarch happened to be passing by. He told them: "This flax weighs three pounds."

Also important in Buddhism is The Middle Way of practicing non-extremism, of hewing to a moderate path between the opposing poles of (depending on the type of Buddhism you practice) either pleasure and pain, liberalism and conservatism, "tastes great" and "less filling," homosexuality and heterosexuality, or Paula Abdul and MC Skat Kat.

> Shogen asked: "Why does the enlightened man not stand on his feet and explain himself?"
>
> And he also said: "This flax weighs three pounds."

Some young Buddhist boys become monks, which means that they shave their heads, live in monasteries, wear brightly-colored robes, take decades-long vows of silence, eschew sex, and learn deadly fighting skills. The most famous Buddhist monks are probably Liu Kang (special attack: "Flying Bicycle Kick") and Kung Lao (special attack: "Hat Throw"), with whom you should be intimately familiar if (like me) you spent the majority of college playing *Mortal Kombat II*.

> Zuigan called out to himself every day: "Master."
>
> Then he answered himself: "Yes, sir."
>
> And after that he added: "This flax weighs three pounds."

Although he is not the official head of Buddhism, the Dalai Lama is perhaps the world's most prominent Buddhist (except possibly for *Pretty Woman* star Richard Gere), on account of his role as spiritual leader of Tibet. There have actually been fourteen Dalai Lamas so far; each time one dies, the Other Lamas visit a holy lake to receive visions of his reincarnation, at which point they kidnap an infant (or occasionally a toddler) and raise him to believe he is the reincarnated Dalai Lama. The current Dalai Lama ("Jetsun Jamphel Ngawang Lobsang Yeshe Tenzin Gyatso") preaches that Buddhism is pro-Communism, anti-gay-sex, and ambivalent toward abortion, which helps, doesn't help, and might or might not help explain why Buddhism has become so popular in California.

> Tanzan wrote sixty postal cards on the last day of his life, and asked an attendant to mail them. Then he passed away.
>
> The cards read: "This flax weighs three pounds."

Buddhists group together in schools, the two largest being Theravada and Mahayana. These schools differ on obscure points of Buddhist theology (e.g. "How many would-be Buddhas are there?" and "How much wood would a would-be Buddha chuck if a would-be Buddha could chuck wood?") but mostly exist to facilitate team sports like Capture the Flag and Red Rover at Buddhist retreats.

> When Eshun, the Zen nun, was past sixty and about to leave this world, she asked some monks to pile up wood in the yard.
>
> Seating herself firmly in the center of the funeral pyre, she had it set fire around the edges.
> "O nun!" shouted one monk, "is it hot in there?"
>
> Eshun answered: "This flax weighs three pounds."

Now, apart from the claims of placemats (which I have found utterly unreliable ever since a McDonalds tray-liner erroneously suggested I could "Super-Size my way to the Super Bowl"), there is no evidence for a cycle of rebirth, for the existence of karma, for the belief that a magic lake can identify the next great spiritual leader, or for the benefits of a bizarre obsession with flax.

We can only conclude that Buddhism is false.

16

Sikhism is false

If you have seen the *Star Wars* prequels, you should be pretty familiar with the Sikhs, who unlike the Jedis are devoted to the violence-loving dark side of the force. They are led by Sikh lords, who typically use the title Darth. The primary commandment of Sikhism is the "Rule of Two," mandating that only two Sikh lords can exist at any time. Some of the most famous Sikh lords were Darth Bane, Darth Plagueis, Darth Sidious, Darth Maul, Darth Tyranus, Darth Vader, Darth Caedus, and Darth Krayt.

Over time the religion has changed, and while they are still inclined to violence, these days Sikhs are more likely to carry ceremonial daggers than light sabers, more likely to drive taxicabs than TIE Fighters, and more likely to have their masses of uncut hair piled up under turbans rather than twirled into side-of-the-head Leia-ish "cinnamon buns." What hasn't changed is that Sikhs worship the god Waheguru, who (conveniently) has no form and cannot be detected by natural means.

The ten gurus

Sikhism originated with the teachings of Guru Nanak Dev, who is most famous for his Yogi-Berra-ish assertion "Realization of Truth is higher than all else. Higher still is truthful living." He also taught "There is no Hindu, there is no Muslim," which ought to come as a pretty big surprise to everyone living in India and Pakistan today. He was followed by nine more gurus with comical names like Angad Dev and Ram Das and Har Rai.

Granth Sahib

The tenth guru, Gobind Singh, couldn't decide who should be guru next, so he instead named Granth Sahib, the Sikh holy scriptures, as his successor.

The Granth Sahib identifies five evils that all devout Sikhs must struggle to avoid:

1. *Sat* (truthful living) stops you from enjoying a good fantasy life.
2. *Santhokh* (contentment) prevents the innovation that leads to economic growth and prosperity.
3. *Daya* (compassion) makes it very easy for charlatans and politicians to take advantage of you.
4. *Nimrata* (humility) leads to awkward, time-wasting "no, *you're* more deserving" arguments.
5. *Pyare* (being filled with the love of god) causes self-righteousness and tiresome sanctimony.

These evils are counterbalanced by the five virtues that Sikhs strive to embody:

1. *Kam* (lust) helps ensure the existence of the next generation of Sikhs.
2. *Krodh* (rage) enables young Sikhs to start heartfelt rock bands like Granth Funk Railroad, The Palki Heads, The Rumala Stones, and Lynyrd Sahib.
3. *Lobh* (greed) recognizes Adam Smith's observation that "[i]t is not from the benevolence of the butcher, the brewer, or the baker that we expect our dinner, but from their regard to their own interest."
4. *Moh* (attachment) allows babies to form bonds with their mothers.
5. *Ahankar* (ego) mediates between the id and super-ego, allowing for the satisfaction of one's urges in long-term-healthy ways.

The five K's

The everyday practice of Sikhism involves five fundamental rules created by Nanak Dev, all of which start with the letter K to make them easier to remember. (Unfortunately, when you write them in English, they don't start with K, and you end up having to lug this book around with you in order to keep track of them.)

uncut hair: Sikhs are forbidden from cutting their hair, due to the mistaken belief that doing so would cause them to lose their superhuman strength.

wooden combs: Sikhs are required to wear wooden combs in their hair. In recent years they have been outcompeted by the Rastafari, who have embraced the cheaper plastic hair picks.

special underwear: Like Mormons, Sikhs are supposed to wear specially-designed underwear, to encourage dignity, modesty, honor, and pretending to be Superman.

iron bracelets: Sikhs are commonly allergic to nickel and silver, and therefore have to resort to wearing iron jewelry.

the sword: Religious Sikhs carry the sword (or dagger) *Kirpan* with them everywhere, as part of their Granth-Sahib-required duty to set off metal detectors and confuse TSA agents.

Sikhs typically wrap their long hair inside a turban, so that it won't get in the way while they are driving their taxicabs. In addition to the 5-K requirements, Sikhs are not allowed to drink or use drugs, and are forbidden from eating either kosher or halal meat, out of fear that the heavy ritual salting might aggravate their hypertension.

Of course, there is no such thing as Waheguru, compassion and humility can (on rare occasions) actually be virtues, haircuts are a lot of fun (especially if your barber has comic books in his lobby and gives out sticks of Juicy Fruit when he's done), and (as was made clear in *Raiders of the Lost Ark*) swords are no match for guns. Sikhism, then, despite its virtues, is false.

17

Jainism is false

No one quite knows when Jainism began, and the Jains aren't particularly helpful, claiming that Jainism has "always" existed. ("Before human beings?" "That's right, before human beings." "Before the rise of vertebrates?" "That's right, before the rise of vertebrates." "Before the emergence of multi-cellular organisms?" "That's right, before the emergence of multi-cellular organisms." "Before the formation of the earth?" "That's right, before the formation of the earth." "Before the birth of the solar system?" "That's right, before the birth of the solar system." "Before the big bang?" "Umm...")

Ahimsa and its karmic consequences

Jainism is rooted in ahimsa, or nonviolence. If you live in America you are probably most familiar with the wimpy Berkeley flavor of nonviolence that revolves around street-puppeteering, freeway-sitting, folk-music vigils, teach-ins, love-ins, sex-ins, sleep-ins, sick-ins, pray-ins, Mary Popp-ins, general strikes, hunger strikes, called third strikes, guerilla theatre, and Rage Against the Machine concerts.

Unlike those dirty hippies, Jains practice an extreme nonviolence that forbids eating meat, swallowing flies, swallowing spiders to catch the flies, using antibiotics to kill bacteria, kicking anthills, shooting bottle rockets at squirrels, gopher-gassing, crop-dusting, building a better mousetrap, huntin' varmints, pied-piping, drilling holes in trees and filling them with herbicide, bullfighting, cockfighting, dogfighting, and babyfighting. The most devout Jains walk around naked, avoid making eye-contact with plants, and eat nothing but rocks and snow.

Jainism teaches that failure to adhere to ahimsa can have "karmic" consequences. For instance, one who kills a man just to watch him die is (according to Jain theology) much more likely himself (either in this life or in a future life) to be killed just to be watched die. Similarly, someone who uses a vacuum cleaner to suck up a giant spider lurking in his bathroom is likely to be afflicted with leprosy. On the flipside, one who continually sweeps the ground in front of him (to lessen the chance of accidentally stepping on a beetle) is karmically much more likely to win at Powerball, to survive a plane crash, to prevail in a frivolous lawsuit, or to or to be reincarnated as Hugh Hefner.

Mahavira

The Jains trace their roots back to a series of twenty-four Jinas, enlightened giants who mostly lived millions of years ago. The religion proper was started by Mahavira, the last Jina, who starved himself to death around the year 500 B.C. Not content with promoting the joy-killing ahimsa, Mahavira forbade other enjoyable pursuits like lying, stealing, sensual pleasure, and possessing things (which seems like it should implicitly forbid stealing, although Mahavira thought it worth his while to forbid them separately). As a result, Jainism caught on much more slowly than it otherwise might have.

Mahavira also taught the important-to-Jainism concepts of *Anekantavada*, the idea we can learn a lot about peaceful coexistence from the example of six blind men groping an elephant, and *Syadvada*, the idea that we can learn a lot about making predictions from the example of six blind men groping an elephant. Elephant-groping is now illegal in most countries, which has resulted in a number of entertaining religious-freedom lawsuits involving Jains.

Jain monks are required to go through life celibate, naked, and poor, and are also required to pluck out their hairs individually in lieu of haircuts or shaving. As a result, the monastic life is not very popular among Jains, except with a handful of masochistic exhibitionists. When Jains get too old, they are supposed to starve themselves to death, following the example of Mahavira. (Some scholars suggest that Karen Carpenter was for this reason a Jain, but most agree that it is more likely that she was a Methodist.)

However, it is clear that celibate, naked, and poor is no way to go through life, that blind men should probably not grope elephants, that there is no connection between pesticide and leprosy, and that ahimsa is a real downer. It is therefore clear that Jainism is false.

18

Zoroastrianism is false

The first draft of this chapter swiftly debunked Zoroastrianism by providing incontrovertible evidence that Don Diego de la Vega, more commonly known as Zorro, never even existed but is in fact the fictional creation of American writer Johnston McCulley, whose series of novellas about the masked anti-hero was not only largely responsible for the American optimism of the Roaring 1920's but also the inspiration for many popular Prohibition-Era drinks, including the Bloody Zorro, the Sour Apple Zorro-tini, the Zorro Collins, and the One-Balled Dictator [Whose Other Ball Was Cut Off By Zorro]. After reading this draft, my editor angrily informed me that Zoroastrianism had absolutely nothing to do with Zorro, and refused to listen to my "it's not my fault they gave it such a misleading name" objections, insisting that I return to the library (I decided not to correct her assumption that I had been there in the first place) and research a proper debunking.

Zoroastrianism was perhaps the first monotheistic religion, and was named after its founder, Zoroaster. As his birth certificate was stolen in what was one of the first historical instances of identity theft, we can only state definitively that Zoroaster (or Zarathustra, as his friends spake him) was born sometime between 6000 B.C. and 600 B.C. in Persia (close to modern-day Kansas City). His name translates as Unfiltered Camel, which was the brand of cigarettes his mother smoked while pregnant with him.

The poetry of Zoroaster

Zoroastrian scripture is based on a series of poems Zoroaster wrote for his high school literary magazine, *Gathas*. These poems addressed the one god Ahura Mazda, whom scholars suspect Zoroaster subconsciously named after a "Star Trek" character and his first car. (This would also help explain the Zoroastrian creed "Zoom zoom.")

SOME POEMS OF ZOROASTER

"Asha"
There's just one Ahura (called Mazda),
And if you respect him he'll cause ya
    Asha (truth and order)
    While you're a supporter,
But once you insult him, he'll toss ya!

"Beaky Buzzard"
Leave corpses on big Silent Towers,
And you'll find in a couple of hours
    They'll get eaten by vultures,
    Then (unlike other cultures)
We'll get all sorts of magical powers.

"Canned Bads"
Your poet's been me, Zoroaster,
And you have to admit I'm the master
    Of divine revelation,
    So don't show hesitation,
Or I'll open a can of disaster.

Rod McKuen he was not. Nonetheless, critical standards were lower several millennia ago; moreover, most early converts were Zoroaster's relatives, who hung his poems on their fridges despite their lack of poetic merit.

Zoroastrianism was popular in Iran for many centuries, until the country was conquered by the Muslims, who forced the Zoroastrians to wear funny costumes, labeled them ritually unclean, and barred them from participating in "reindeer games." As a result, many Iranian Zoroastrians converted to Islam, many more moved to India and rebranded themselves as Parsis and became flamboyant lead singers for Queen, and a handful stuck around and attempted to use their persecution to get sympathy dates.

The practice of Zoroastrianism

Zoroaster summed up his morality as "good thoughts, good words, good deeds" after focus-grouping a number of poorly-received alternatives, including "good, good, good, good vibrations," "no gnews is good gnews," and "temporary lay offs, good times, easy credit rip offs, good times, scratchin' and surviving, good times."

Devout Zoroastrians wear the *kushti*, a sacred girdle designed to help believers maintain their girlish figures, and the *sedreh*, "the epitome of rumpledness and related virtues–relaxed fit, robber-baron look, with squared-off demi-patch pocket, seven-button placket, and two-button adjustable cuffs. The sleeves have a way of highlighting the strength of a man's arms, even if he is the sort of man who rarely lifts more than a calculator. Paired with a suit jacket, it's Detroit. Or maybe Mecca. Classic fit. Debonair, friable, diaphanous. And momentous. You'll fit right in in busy Tijuana at 2 a.m., looking for some interesting trouble."

Zoroastrians believe that, after death, one's soul can only be freed if his body is left on a "Tower of Silence" and eaten by vultures. In many Zoroastrian-heavy parts of the world, however, vultures are on their way to extinction, largely (and ironically) on account of overeating. As a result, Zoroastrian corpses are going longer and longer without being eaten, which is both creating rat problems and lowering property values in most Zoroastrian neighborhoods. It is possible that, within a few years, vultures may go extinct, after which no Zoroastrian soul will *ever* be free, unless they change their doctrines and give soul-freeing powers to rats, maggots, chipmunks, donkeys, monkeys, beetles, dogs, crows, chickens, elephants, or the homeless.

Zoroastrians worship at fire temples in a ceremony known as "arson." (Non-Zoroastrians are prohibited from observing the sacred fires, which means we sort of have to take their word for what's really going on inside. It's certainly possible that they're just sitting around, drinking pints of *Yazata* or *Yazata* Light or *Yazata* Dry or *Yazata* Ice or *Yazata* Ultra, and telling jokes about non-Zoroastrians: "How many non-Zoroastrians does it take to get eaten by vultures?" "None, those chumps stick their dead bodies under the ground like chumps, and they *never* get eaten by vultures, and their souls *never* get freed!" "Ha, ha, ha, good one, Zubin!")

But unless your name is Beavis or Butthead, there is nothing sacred about fire. Also, it's disgusting and unsanitary to leave corpses for birds to eat, and bad poetry is no evidence for the supernatural. Zoroastrianism is false.

19

Bahá'í is false

In 1844, a Persian named Báb decided that he was the Shia Mahdi, the Zoroastrian Ushídar-Máh, the Jewish prophet Elijah, John the Baptist, the Buddha, Confucius, Birdman, Yoda, and Joseph Smith. Due to the ludicrousness of these claims, he was executed by firing squad and fed to animals.

Bahá'u'lláh, the most outgoing of Báb's followers, grabbed the reins of Bábism, quickly proclaimed himself the all-messiah, and rebranded the faith as Bahá'i (from the Arabic *Bahá*, meaning "a peninsula in western Mexico"). After posing for a famous photograph and writing a series of humorous "Lazlo Letters" to world leaders and corporate officials, Bahá'u'lláh died of a fever and was buried in the holy Shrine of Bahá'u'lláh.

Bahá'ís believe that all religions are sort of true, and that god is both incomprehensible and best understood as a weighted average of Yahweh, Allah, Ahura Mazda, Xenu, Ganesh, Make-Make, Lolth, and Al Gore. They are also avid supporters of multiculturalism (the idea that people will get a better education if they're surrounded by a wide variety of not-very-bright classmates) and Esperanto (a fake language invented by a Russian ophthalmologist to destroy the evils of multilingualism).

Being Bahá'í

Bahá'ís are required to pray once a day, although they have a choice of three prayers depending on how busy they are:

short: "Hey, god, you're great and I suck."

medium: same as the short prayer, but repeated three times

long: repeat "Alláh-u-Abhá" enough times that it loses all meaning

Bahá'ís are forbidden from begging, being gay, setting things on fire in order to collect insurance money, shaving their heads, libel, slander, and sexting. They are also supposed to fast for the entirety of March Madness, even though no Bahá'í university has ever made it out of the round of 64.

Today there are more than 5 million Bahá'ís, who live all over the world and follow the teachings of United-Nations-sounding institutions like the Spiritual Assembly, the Regional Councils, the Shoghi Effendi, and the International House of Justice (where I recommend trying the funny-face pancakes).

However, as the various religions are clearly incompatible, as March Madness is a great time for snacking with your friends, and as multiculturalism is an unmitigated evil, the Bahá'í faith is false.

20

Feng Shui is false

Feng Shui is the ancient Chinese practice of re-arranging your furniture, using The Laws of Heaven and Earth, to promote a positive flow of qi ("kwee"), a Chinese concept that refers to either energy, joie de vivre, lifebreath, vigour, verve, subtle energy, vim, élan vital, or harmony. (Mostly, though, it means "vim.") Practitioners claim that making choices according to the dictates of Feng Shui will produce results that are auspicious, i.e. "in accord with the dictates of Feng Shui."

Feng Shui literally means "wind-water," an allusion to a quote from Guo Pu's *Zhangshu*: "Qi rides the wind and scatters, but also retains water."

Feng Shui is commonly used to choose locations for homes and graves, to schedule planned C-sections, and to create cleverly-named paint schemes for new car models (like Tambora Flame Metallic and British Racing Green and Kwee Brown). Feng Shui stores catering to the profoundly gullible sell everything from feng shui measuring tapes (with auspicious lengths prominently marked), to feng shui belts (with auspicious holes prominently marked), to feng shui televisions (with auspicious channels prominently marked).

Although there are many Feng Shui techniques, the following are some of the most common:

Wu Xing: creating a balance between the five elements of the Chinese periodic table: Wood, Fire, Earth, Metal, and Water. (Chinese people are not very good at chemistry, it turns out.)

Time and Space: involves repeated play of feng shui master Leon Russell's "Stop All That Jazz" album.

Shooting Stars: can be used to make wishes that (purely coincidentally) sometimes come true.

Eight Mansions: is a large enough number that at least one of them should be auspicious. Then you can sell the rest.

Nine Palaces: similar to Eight Mansions but slightly more luxurious.

Hemerology: often results in bright red blood in the toilet bowl.

You can see that none of these techniques actually tells you *what* to do, which forces the poor Feng Shui believer to hire expensive Feng Shui consultants (or take expensive Feng Shui courses) in order not to mis-qi his living room.

Case study: choosing a house

Based on consultations with a certified and accredited Feng Shui master, I compiled the following qi-rific rules you might consider next time you move.

1. Do not live near a church, or you will find it difficult to find parking on Sundays and might even get your driveway blocked.
2. Do not live near a crack house, because evil energy hovers there.
3. Do not live near an airport, as you might get in trouble for your hobby of shining lasers into the sky.
4. Do not live near a hospital, because you might get germs.
5. Do not live within 500 feet of an elementary school, as that would violate the terms of your parole agreement.
6. Do not live at the end of a dead-end street, as an inattentive driver might end up in your living room.
7. Do not live near an Indian restaurant, or everything will reek of curry whenever you open your windows.

You can see that pretty much all of the teachings of Feng Shui are either common sense, superstitions, delusions, misconceptions, falsehoods, fabrications, or judgments of aesthetics. In any event, they have nothing to do with qi (which does not exist), and so Feng Shui is false.

Taoism is false

Taoism began around 3500 years ago with the ancient Chinese sage Laozi ("lousy"). Despite the initial T, it is properly pronounced *D*aoism, which you would do well to remember if you don't want to get laughed out of the monastery like I did.

Tao

Taoism revolves around the concept of Tao, which is Chinese for "Dao." Tao is traditionally considered to be indescribable, which makes writing this chapter sort of difficult. Tao has no shape or form, is both still and moving, and is both larger than Oprah Winfrey and smaller than Gary Coleman. Tao is also often considered to be like water, in the sense that it is flavorless and odorless, and also because it makes you need to pee.

Taoists believe that Tao signifies the true nature of the world: nasty, brutish, and short. (French Taoists often insist that this is instead the true nature of *Napoleon*, but other Taoists tend to ignore them on this topic.) Tao does both everything and nothing, is responsible for both being and non-being, feels both warm and cold, tastes both sweet and bitter, and makes both sense and no sense (mostly, however, no sense).

The *Tao Te Ching*

The concept of Tao was introduced by Laozi in his classic *Tao Te Ching* ("The Classic/Canon of the Way/Path and the Power/Virtue"), a collection of 81 short poems about timeless themes like ineffability, valley spirits, the products of not-being, and spokes. The *Tao Te Ching* makes a number of unverifiable assertions about Tao:

- Tao is subtle. (Which is probably not surprising, given that it doesn't actually exist.)
- Tao is quiet. (Incongruously, Tao is also loud.)

- Tao is Master Shen's younger brother and a highly skilled assassin-for-hire. (This shouldn't be news to anyone who watches "Dragon Ball Z.")
- Tao is like a well. (Children often fall into it.)

The practice of Taoism

Taoists try to follow the "three jewels" of compassion, frugality, and aquamarine. (Although she is often associated with Taoism on account of her frequent attempts to write bad *Tao Te Ching*-ish poetry, Jewel Kilcher is not in fact one of the Taoist jewels.)

Other important Taoist concepts include *Te* (which means either "power," "virtue," "ascension," "integrity," "graciousness," "good government," "objectivity," "purpose," "beginning," "phoenix-head," "tree-planting," or "Republic of Germany," giving Taoists wide latitude in their religious practice), *Wu Wei* ("creative quietude"), and *Pu* (a bear "of little brain" who loves "hunny").

Yin and Yang

Taoism's most well-known symbol is probably the black-and-white-swirly Yin Yang, which represents either "change, the only constant in the universe," sexual harassment, racial harmony, two tadpoles trying to sniff each other's butts, simultaneous oral sex, or the Pink Floyd album *Dark Side of the Moon.*

Common Taoist practices include eating, fasting, fortune-telling, parades, burning pictures of things that "spirits" might need, reading, and tai chi.

In lieu of medical treatment, sick Taoists often opt for chi nei tsang, a deep belly massage that "reorganizes internal tissues and energies" in order to "bring Yin and Yang back into balance." Unlike modern medicines that were probably developed by doctors and scientists funded by profit-seeking pharmaceutical companies, chi nei tsang was created by Taoist monks who lived in the mountains of China and whose integrity was beyond reproach. (Their judgment, on the other hand, is completely suspect, primarily because they were Taoist monks.)

But as modern medicine is occasionally helpful, as bad poetry is never evidence of ineffability, and as nothing is larger than Oprah Winfrey, Taoism is false.

Confucianism is false

Confucius was an ancient Chinese philosopher who taught a system of morality premised on bad puns, sexual and scatological wordplay, and stereotypes of immigrant-poor English grammar. His teachings were codified in the *Analects of Confucius* several hundred years after his death and serve today as the basis of the Confucianist religion, which is practiced by millions of people in East Asia.

Confucius say...

Unlike other Asian religions, Confucianism is reasonably well-known in the West, mostly because Confucius's pithy religious pronouncements are popular staples of children's joke books:

- If you want pretty nurse, you got to be patient
- To meet girl in park is good, to park meat in girl is better
- Panties not best thing on earth, but next to it
- Man who go to bed with itchy butt, wake up with smelly finger
- Women who go camping, must beware of evil intent
- Man standing on toilet, is high on pot
- Man who walk through airport door sideways, going to Bangkok
- Man who try to eat family photo soon spitting image of father
- Man with hand in pocket feel cocky all day

The new Confucianism

After decades of disfavor, a New Confucianism in which karaoke, action movies, and call girls play a prominent role is gaining popularity in China. And it is true that singing, martial arts, and sex are widely regarded as the three elements of a successful birthday party. Nonetheless, the last time I was in an airport, I walked sideways through the door and ended up not in Bangkok but in Burbank. Likewise, I once met a pretty nurse when I was not the slightest bit sick (although I had to wait a long time, for some reason). Therefore Confucianism is quite false.

Shinto is false

Shinto, once the official religion of Japan, has in recent years (through mismanagement and a series of poor investments) become the unofficial religion of Japan. While the word *shinto* is difficult to translate into English, we can be reasonably confident that it means either "the way of the gods," "the way from the gods," or "away from the gods."

Shinto revolves around the worship of kami, which are a collection of gods, spirits, ghosts, ghouls, goblins, Pokémon, meteorological phenomena, mountains, animals, and robot lions that can combine to form a giant man-shaped robot. The following are probably the most famous kami:

- Pikachu
- Mount Fuji
- Hurricane Katrina
- Green Lion
- Antonio Inoki
- George Takei
- the Sun Goddess Amaterasu
- Emperor Hirohito (possibly)
- Boo Berry
- Godzilla (but not Godzuki)

However, pretty much anything can become a kami as long as enough Shintoists request it. If there are any Shintoists who haven't already put the book down in disgust, it's always sort of been a dream of mine to be a kami (and also to meet Pikachu). Thanks, guys.

Ten precepts and four affirmations

Like many other religions, Shinto contains ten commandments, although it calls them precepts in order to make them sound less unpleasant. They include admonitions to call your grandmother, to do whatever a kami tells you, and to be wary of foreigners. These precepts are not particularly useful or interesting, although learning about them might help you make sense of your Japan vacation, of the "Monchichi" episode "Misfit Grumplin," and of a number of otherwise-incomprehensible Gwen Stefani videos.

In case you don't do well with specific advice, Shinto also has four vague affirmations that it recommends you think about:

1. Tradition. (As opposed to all those other religions that eschew tradition.)
2. Nature. (Is considered sacred on account of containing kami.)
3. Obsessive cleanliness. (Shintoists are required to brush their teeth at least twice a day, to wash their hands after every visit to the bathroom, and to sneeze into tissues rather than their sleeves.)
4. Kami-worship festivals (These often include parades, carnival rides, haunted houses, ring tosses, weight-guessers, funnel cakes, drift-wood sculptures, deep-fried Twinkies, and petting zoos.)

Shintoists are obsessed with purity, and Shinto priests will typically conduct purification rituals not only during relocations of kami shrines, but also before the first production run at any new Toyota factory, whenever a sushi restaurant replaces its conveyor belt, at the release party for each new *Yu-Gi-Oh!* booster pack, and at preview screenings of new Miyazaki movies.

As mentioned earlier, there are no official requirements for Shintos. Nonetheless, over the years Shintoists have developed common practices including *ema* (donating pictures of horses to shrines in order to pacify spirits), *kagura* (participating in reality-TV dance contests in order to pacify spirits), and *collectivism* (collectivism).

However, since there are no such things as kami, since deep-fried Twinkies are exceptionally unhealthy, and since purity is vastly overrated (except for the *Reinheitsgebot*), Shinto is false.

RELIGIONS OF THE JEWS

24

The story of the Jews

Judaism was the first great monotheistic religion. (Zoroastrianism may have been earlier, but it was never all that great.) The Jews worship a god known by a variety of names, including G-d (mostly among worshippers playing Hangman), Adonai ("my lord"), Elohim ("that angry dude in the sky who's always trying to kill us"), and Yahweh (after the Michael McDonald song "Yah Weh B There").

Euphemisms for god

Religious Jews believe it is disrespectful to speak or write their god's name and have adopted an elaborate collection of euphemisms to refer to him:

- "Hashem"
- "Colonel Goddo"
- "Gee Oh Double Dizzle"
- "Big Poppa Pump"
- "Dog Backwards"
- "Old Man You-Know-Who"
- "Doctor Goddenstein"
- "The Shogun of Harlem"
- "Geraldine"
- "Odd-gay"

The story of creation

Jewish theology is laid out in the Old Testament, which is divided into two sections: The Torah and That Other Stuff. According to these scriptures, the Jewish god created the world about 5800 years ago, which helps explain why observant Jews regularly show up to work several billion years late. This creation story, shared by both Christians and Muslims, is sufficiently well-known that I feel comfortable giving you just the highlights:

Day 1: God creates light, day, night. First "Take Back the Night" march is held.

Day 2: God creates the firmament, a hemisphere over the (flat) earth with a series of openings for the sun and moon (not yet created) to move through.

Day 3: God creates the land and the sea, trees and plants and fruits. Flowers spend most of the day wondering who's going to pollinate them and how they're going to photosynthesize.

Day 4: God creates incandescent lights and hangs them from the firmament as stars. Also creates sun (on purpose) and moon (by mistake). Flowers still not being pollinated.

Day 5: God creates birds and fish. Fish rejoice that there are no bears or seals to eat them. Birds likewise rejoice at lack of cats.

Day 6: God creates bears and seals and cats. Also, Adam and Eve.

Day 7: God stays in bed all day watching college football.

This story raises more questions than it answers. How could day and night be created three days before the sun? As a college football fan, does god support the BCS system or a playoff or neither? Also, lights hanging from the firmament? Holes for the sun and moon? Really, holes? This is what's keeping people from believing in evolution? Are you sure you're not pulling my leg?

The rest of the story you are probably familiar with: snake tricks Adam and Eve into eating the wrong fruit, leading to expulsion from paradise. Adam and Eve have lots of children. Incest is invented. Cain kills Abel, starts first heavy-metal band Brother's Keeper, tours the world. Mankind turns wicked; Noah builds arky-arky to survive floody-floody. Attempted sky-tower results in jumbling of languages and first debates over bilingual education. Abraham is born, circumcises self, stops enjoying sex.

Abraham

Now, in Abraham's time, idol-worship was common, and Abraham's father owned Mesopotamian Idol, a small but thriving retail store that (according to rabbinic commentary) invented the Presidents Day Sale. One day, after the young Abraham begin hearing voices commanding him to destroy things, he smashed up his father's inventory with a tire iron, which he then left in the hands of one of the few unbroken idols. His father, as you might expect, refused to believe that an idol could have come to life and destroyed other idols. "If idols can't even destroy other idols," pointed out Abraham, "then how can they be worthy gods? Join me instead in worshipping Colonel Goddo, the invisible sky-man!" As every parent knows, it is nearly impossible to productively argue theology with a seven-year-old, so Abraham's dad gave in, and Judaism began.

Abraham is considered the father not only of Judaism (through his direct descendants) and Islam (through a bastard child he had with the cleaning lady) but also of nutjob religious extremism, as he was the first person ever to attempt a "god told me to" filicide. At the last minute, god relented and let Abraham kill a goat instead, but the psychological scars left on his son Isaac trickled down for several generations, to his son Jacob (who tricked his brother Esau out of his inheritance for a bowl of just-right porridge), to his son Joseph (who dressed flamboyantly and faked his own death and relocated the entire Jewish family to Egypt, where they were promptly enslaved and forced to build pyramids full of secret chambers, hieroglyphic murals, scorpion kings, murderous traps, hidden treasures, snake pits, and mummy's curses).

Moses

Eventually the ruling Pharaoh (who had something of a thing for Jewish women) decreed that all Jewish boys must be drowned in the river, leaving every Sarah, Rachel, and Leah ripe for his advances. One Jewish boy, Charlton Heston (or "Moses"), was floated down the river by his mother, at which point he was rescued by a skinny-dipping Egyptian princess and raised as a royal orphan. After an adolescent killing spree, Moses fled into the desert, where a severe case of heatstroke led him to hallucinate that a burning bush was speaking to him. He returned to Egypt, demanded that the Pharaoh free the Jews, and then loosed ten horrific plagues on the Egyptians after Pharaoh refused:

1. Blood: All Egyptian women bleed from uterus once a month.
2. Frogs: Egypt overrun by French tourists.
3. Lice: Egyptian children banned from school until treated, fall behind in global math and science rankings, never catch up.
4. Wild Animals: Dig through Egyptian trash cans, make huge, smelly mess.
5. Mad Cow Disease: Leads to economy-crippling Japanese import ban on Egyptian beef.
6. Boils: Knock early favorite Miss Egypt out of Miss Flat Earth contest.
7. Fiery Hail: Puts fiery dents in Egyptian chariots; insurance refuses to cover "act of god."

8. Locusts: Destroy biofuel crops then vanish before Egyptians can pickle and eat them.
9. Darkness: Egyptians look directly at missing sun, damage retinas irreparably.
10. Death of the Firstborn: Egyptian elite compete to hold gaudiest funeral, go broke.

While the Egyptians were busy holding wakes and visiting ophthalmologists, the Jews took off and crossed the mysteriously-parted Red Sea (so called on account of its eerie blue color), which promptly un-parted and drowned the pursuing Egyptians, whose lingering vision problems prevented them from finding their way back to shore. (Also, they couldn't swim.) The Jews complained about being hungry and water-thirsty and blood-thirsty, until Moses found them manna (nutritious psychoactive mushrooms), produced water by hitting a rock, and ordered eternal war against the Amalekites, who today are known as "atheists" or "freethinkers" or "the sensible."

After a brief-but-bloody killing spree, the Israelites showed up at Mount Sinai, where Yahweh bashfully handed them a note asking if they would be his "chosen people." After discussing it with their school-friends, they blushingly accepted.

In dire need of a vacation, Moses ate a double helping of mind-altering manna and climbed the mountain to receive the Ten Commandments. (It ended up being kind of a lousy vacation, although not as bad as the time you went to Tijuana, got duped into watching the sex show with the girl and the donkey, and ended up spending the night in jail.)

The Ten Commandments

Due to a calculation error, there are actually twelve commandments. By the time this was discovered, movie posters for *The Ten Commandments* had already been printed, and so (in order to avoid a costly reprint) to this day we still pretend that there are only ten.

Redneck lawmakers often claim that the ten commandments are the basis for the American justice system, and hillbilly judges likewise sometimes insist on installing replica copies of the commandments in their courtrooms. However, depending on whether you are in Mississippi or not, only three or four of the commandments represent actual crimes: murder, theft, perjury, and (maybe) adultery. Most of the rest represent just the type of religious gobbledygook that forced the writing of this book.

1. I am god
2. No other gods
3. No making idols
4. Don't use god's name wrongfully
5. Celebrate the sabbath

These first five are what Biblical scholars often call the "domestic violence" commandments, as they are eerily similar to the hyper-controlling restrictions used by abusers in dysfunctional relationships: "Don't look at other men!" "Did I say you could talk to your friends?!" "It's after sunset on a Friday! Why the hell isn't dinner ready yet?!"

As you can see, none of these is related in the slightest to our modern legal system, unless you live in Paramus, New Jersey, where "worldly employment" is forbidden on Sundays; in Georgia, where buying liquor is illegal on the sabbath; in Arkansas, which has an entire prison for idolators; or in Massachusetts, where it is a crime to "wilfully blaspheme the holy name of God by denying, cursing or contumeliously reproaching God, his creation, government or final judging of the world."

6. Honor your parents

Although the Jews mostly believed that all twelve commandments were given to Moses by their god, they always secretly wondered whether this commandment was actually added by Moses himself, as his sons Gershom and Eliezer were disrespectful hoodlums who had ignored all previous attempts at discipline. Parent-dishonor is currently legal in all fifty states and in most territories as well.

7. Don't murder

As god had, only a couple of chapters earlier, ordered the Jews to murder the Amalekites, everyone agreed that this commandment was probably best ignored.

8. No adultery

As god had, in the preceding book, watched with lecherous approval while Abraham knocked up his wife's maid, everyone agreed that this commandment was probably best ignored.

> 9. Don't steal

The Jews begged Moses to clarify whether downloading the new Matisyahu album off the internet counted (in a Twelve Commandments sense) as stealing, but he refused to answer, explaining that the internet was several millennia in the future (and that anyway he hated reggae).

> 10. Don't bear false witness

Unless, of course, you are doing so to convince your father that he shouldn't worship idols and should instead throw his allegiance to Doctor Goddenstein, in which case you're allowed.

> 11. Don't covet your neighbor's house
> 12. Don't covet your neighbor's wife

These last two are at least good practical advice, as coveting often leads to staring, and once your neighbor sees you staring at his wife all day, he's probably going to kick your ass. You'd be better off coveting one of the wives who lives over on Cedar Hill, since all those houses are surrounded by trees that provide lots of cover for aspiring peeping-toms (or so I have heard). Nonetheless, coveting is currently legal pretty much everywhere.

The golden calf

Moses took longer than expected to bring back these commandments, and he didn't bother to call, so eventually the Israelites started to worry that he wasn't coming back. Despite their first-hand experience with Yahweh's murderous nature and emotional fragility, they inexplicably insisted that Moses's brother Aaron create them a new, calf-shaped god out of gold jewelry. Moses (barely) managed to talk Yahweh out of completely exterminating the calf-worshippers, but he burned the gold (chemically impossible), ground it into dust (chemically impossible), dissolved it in water (chemically impossible), and forced them to drink it (chemically possible).

After this Moses callously ordered the massacre of thousands of Jews, and Yahweh loosed a plague (probably hantavirus) on the remainder, until at last they apologized for hurting his feelings. As punishment, god gave them additional, even-more-oppressive commandments (including, among other things, prohibitions on eating pork and cheeseburgers and jumbo prawns and hagfish) and marched them off into the desert. For the next 40 years, they kept on hurting Yahweh's sensitive feelings, he kept coming up with a variety of plans (each more diabolical than the last) to exterminate them, and Moses kept barely talking him out of it.

Israel and the diaspora

Eventually the Jews ditched Moses on top of a mountain and slaughtered their way through Israel, where they built a temple and established a lineage of kings who became famous for consorting with witches, slaying giants, and chopping babies in half. Soon afterward, however, they were conquered by Zoroastrians, who were in turn conquered by the Romans, who destroyed the temple and dispersed the Jews all over the earth, creating a diaspora of Jews who had vastly different experiences in different countries:

Venice: acted as "Shylocks," lending money in exchange for pounds of flesh
France: sold military secrets to 19th-century Germany
Germany: were loaded onto trains and sent to gas chambers
Canada: fronted Ayn-Rand-themed rock band
Sweden: rigged Nobel Prize voting to favor Jewish scientists
UK: invented larger-than-life characters Ali G, Borat, and Bruno
China: became infamous for refusing to eat sciatic nerves
America: dominated entertainment industry until the rise of Scientology

Throughout the years, Jews maintained a belief that Israel was promised to them by god, and that they would return there someday. After World War II, in which Nazi Germany exterminated millions of Jews, the world decided to give them this land as a consolation prize. And there they have built their own Jewish state, on a barren sliver of desert land, surrounded by countries full of heavily-armed people who hate Jews. To no one's great surprise, most Jews (with the exception of those who previously lived in horrible places like Ethiopia and Russia and Detroit) have opted to stick it out in the diaspora.

25

Judaism is false

Jews believe that they are god's "chosen people":

> For thou art an holy people unto the LORD thy God, and the LORD hath chosen thee to be a peculiar people unto himself, above all the nations that are upon the earth.

> Deuteronomy 14:2

To a sensible person, thousands of years of persecution and suffering would be sufficient to demonstrate the silliness of this idea. However, in what is a very common religious trick, Jews choose to take the fact that they could have been persecuted even more than they actually were as demonstration of their chosen-ness.

The Jewish holidays

Jews celebrate Saturday as their sabbath, mostly to force their young men to wear skullcaps and study Torah instead of participating in worldly pursuits like playing college football and watching cartoons and hunting vampires.

In addition to regular-people holidays like Thanksgiving and Presidents Day, Jews celebrate a variety of religious-themed holidays commemorating fictional events important to the Jewish people:

Rosh Hashanah is the Jewish New Year, celebrated on the exact anniversary of the day 6000-ish years ago when god created man.

Yom Kippur (the Day of Atonement) is a time to demonstrate penitence for pissing off god, mostly by groveling and fasting and suffering. Because of demand for this uplifting and popular event, synagogues often require the purchase of expensive tickets for attendance and prohibit worshippers from "rebroadcasts or retransmission without the express written consent of Major League Baseball."

Day About Nothing mourns the end of the "Seinfeld" series.

Chanukah was recently invented to (unsuccessfully) compete with Christmas for mindshare among children, and commemorates a historically-unimportant Jewish civil war several thousand years ago.

Passover celebrates god's tenth-plague genocide of the Egyptians by requiring eight days of a restrictive, cracker-heavy diet.

Yom Ha-Carew commemorates Rod Carew's 3000th hit, on August 4, 1985.

Most Jews also look forward to the arrival of the messiah (from the Hebrew for "oratorio"), who is prophesied to show up, cover himself in anointing oil, and usher in a time of prosperity, peace, and zombie-like resurrection of the dead. The Bible makes many specific predictions about the future messiah, who will be a descendant of King David, will have degree from an Ivy League school (not Brown), will force everyone to worship Colonel Goddo, will destroy all weapons (leading to an ugly conflict with Jews for the Preservation of Firearms Ownership), and will rebuild the Temple in Jerusalem using only Certified Green designs and construction.

Judaism and scholarship

Jews have a long tradition of scholarship, which has produced famous thinkers like Rabbi Akiba ben Joseph, Rabbi Hillel the Elder, Maimonides, Karl Marx, Woody Allen, Milton Friedman, and Paula Abdul. Hillel is most famous for providing a one-sentence explanation of Judaism:

> Once there was a gentile who came before Shammai and said to him: Convert me on the condition that you teach me the whole Torah while I stand on one foot. Shammai pushed him aside with the measuring stick he was holding. The same fellow came before Hillel, and Hillel converted him, saying: That which is despicable to you, do not do to your fellow, this is the whole Torah, and the rest is commentary, go and learn it.

However, as the Torah is filled with examples of despicable behavior, as prohibitions on bacon and cheeseburgers are too unpleasant to be mere "commentary," as there is no Colonel Goddo, and as scientists have conclusively shown that the world is at least ten thousand years old, Judaism is false.

26

Orthodox Judaism is false

Orthodox Jews attempt to follow literally all the rules outlined in the Old Testament of the Bible. This includes dietary laws, fasting laws, laws specifying allowed foods, laws specifying prohibited foods, butchering laws, agricultural laws, ingredient-labeling laws, livestock laws, hunting laws, scavenging laws, gathering laws, cherry-picking laws, and drinking-so-much-until-you-don't-know-the-difference-between-good-and-evil laws.

The practice of Orthodox Judaism

Orthodox Jews take perhaps most seriously the Biblical admonition "You shall not kindle a fire in any of your dwellings on the sabbath day" (Exodus 35:3), refraining from such fire-kindling activities as driving, fire-kindling, pushing elevator buttons, arson, typing, flipping light-switches, re-arranging furniture, creating fragrant scents, opening refrigerator doors, adjusting thermostats, hitting the snooze button, or milking cows.

However, Orthodox Jews believe that god is more interested in the letter than the spirit of the law; accordingly, they have spent the last thousand years inventing technically-kosher ways to engage in sabbath-prohibited activities, including always-on ovens, scheduled pedestrian crossings, milking machines, self-driving cars, pilot lights, monkey butlers, text-to-speech software, opaque lampshades, programmable coffeemakers, and hiring a Black guy.

A popular misconception is that Orthodox Jews are required to have sex through a hole in a sheet. In fact, this is only true for sex with the dead, and the holes are not in sheets, but in specialized burial shrouds called *tachrichim*. Orthodox Jews also refrain from masturbation, based on the fear of ending up like Onan, who disobeyed god's command to impregnate his brother's widow when he "pulled out" and "spilled seed" on the ground, and whom god killed as a result. In addition, Orthodox Jews consider it a grave crime (on par with man-on-man gay sex) for a man to remarry his ex-wife after she has been defiled by another man.

Curiously, Orthodox Judaism does not forbid lesbianism, teaching that "girl-on-girl" action is permissible as long as it is "hot," "steamy," "moist," or "filthy."

Haredi Orthodox vs Modern Orthodox

There are two main groups of Orthodox Jews, the Haredi ("funny hat") Orthodox and the Modern Orthodox. Their primary differences are summed up below:

Haredi Orthodox	Modern Orthodox
name derived from Hebrew *charada*, meaning "fear [of god]"	name derived from Latin *modo*, meaning "[fear of NY Times columnist] Maureen Dowd"
beliefs and practices can be traced directly back to Moses	beliefs and practices can be traced directly back to Joe Lieberman
consider "Ultra-Orthodox" a pejorative term	consider "Ultra-Orthodox" a good DJ name
wear funny hats and black suits	wear stylish yarmulkes with embroidered political slogans
shopping at GAP forbidden	shopping at GAP encouraged
boys and girls attend separate schools	boys and girls attend same schools but have different textbooks
generally hostile to science	only hostile to science when it contradicts the Bible
live in insular, segregated communities with other Haredim	live in insular, segregated communities with other wealthy people
rely on the Modern Orthodox for medical care, script-doctoring, and Congressional representation	rely on the Haredim for good deals on diamond jewelry
love Matisyahu	love Matisyahu more

However, it is pretty clear that the world is full of people who drive on Saturdays, who routinely spill seed inside hollowed-out melons (or so I have heard), and who find Matisyahu completely unlistenable; and that most of these people lead fulfilling, productive, not-smitten-by-god lives. Therefore, Orthodox Judaism must be false.

27

Reform Judaism is false

Most Jewish people these days are Reform Jews, which means they believe that only certain parts of the Old Testament are true. Exactly which parts vary from Jew to Jew, although typically just the parts that are least onerous to comply with are kept.

Reform Jews tend to believe in the existence of the always-pissed Old Testament god, though they are often skeptical of the claim that he created the world in six days, suggesting that (for instance) "maybe each 'day' for god is really like a million years." (If you point out to them that this would mean that plants somehow survived millions of years without sunlight or being pollinated, they will often get angry and cut off your access to capital.)

Reform Jews tend to be somewhat lax about the Bible's dietary restrictions, often insisting that they apply (for example) "when I eat at home, but not when I eat at Bennigan's" or "only when my parents are visiting" or "just on a handful of religious holidays of my own choosing." In addition, Reform Jews eschew Biblical prohibitions on things as varied as tattoos ("Do not cut your bodies for the dead or put tattoo marks on yourselves. I am the LORD!"), homosexuality ("Thou shalt not lie with mankind, as with womankind: it is abomination. I am the LORD!"), suicide ("Your blood which belongs to your souls I will demand; I am the LORD!"), eating vultures and buzzards ("And these you shall regard as an abomination among the birds; they shall not be eaten, they are an abomination: the eagle, the vulture, the buzzard; I am the LORD!"), and mixed-fiber clothing ("Do not wear clothes of wool and linen woven together. I am the LORD!").

Unlike Orthodox prayer services, which are conducted almost entirely in Hebrew, Reform services are often held in English, mime, Okie, Perl, Esperanto, !Kung, Cajun, Klingon, or even Ebonic. They are also likely to involve female rabbis ("rabbettes"), oversized foam novelty hands ("MOSES #1!"), musical accompaniment (often Simon and Garfunkel), dance squads (e.g. the Dallas Cowboys cheerleaders), and audience participation (most commonly the wave).

Intermarriage

The one Biblical rule that Reform Jews take very seriously is the prohibition on intermarriage:

> When the LORD your God brings you into the land you are entering to possess and drives out before you many nations – the Hittites, Girgashites, Amorites, Canaanites, Perizzites, Hivites and Jebusites, seven nations larger and stronger than you – and when the LORD your God has delivered them over to you and you have defeated them, then you must destroy them totally. Make no treaty with them, and show them no mercy. Do not intermarry with them. Do not give your daughters to their sons or take their daughters for your sons, for they will turn your sons away from following me to serve other gods, and the LORD's anger will burn against you and will quickly destroy you.
>
> Deuteronomy 7:1-4

They take it so seriously that they often extend the prohibitions beyond Perizzites and Hivites and Jebusites to include Christians, Buddhists, Muslims, Hindus, and Wiccans. (For some reason they tend to skip over the "destroy them totally" part of the rule.) Reform Jewish parents have in extreme cases been observed to disown their intermarrying children in the hopes of avoiding god's Deuteronomy-promised wrath. However, it is easy to check that history contains no recorded cases of the LORD's anger quickly destroying the parents of intermarriers, demonstrating that this law (like the rest of Reform Judaism) is false.

Kabbalah is false

Kabbalah is the name given to the focus on the mystical aspects of Judaism. If you are wondering what exactly distinguishes the mystical and non-mystical aspects of Judaism, you are not alone, as I myself had to procure the assistance of a rabbinical-school dropout to figure it out. Luckily for you, I came out of the process with a useful cheat sheet:

non-mystical	mystical
wearing yarmulke to demonstrate respect for imaginary god	wearing red string bracelet as protection from imaginary "evil eye"
talking to god	god talking back
searching fictional texts for meaning	searching fictional texts for "inner meaning"
reading holy books as written	treating holy books as cryptograms and subjecting them to man-in-the-middle attacks
avoiding speaking god's name	constructing new names for god by reading the Bible backward
baking braided challah bread to commemorate manna that once fell from heaven	creating golems out of clay to commemorate creation of Adam (from clay)
messing with the Zohar	not messing with the Zohar

Madonna

Kabbalah's most famous proponent is "Material Girl" Madonna, who has a diverse history of religious dalliances with Catholicism ("Like a Prayer"), the pro-choice movement ("Papa Don't Preach"), Astrology ("Lucky Star"), Clapton-worship ("Crazy for You"), Zoroastrianism ("Holiday"), Islam ("Justify my Love"), Hinduism ("Beautiful Stranger"), Juche

("La Isla Bonita"), Mormonism ("Express Yourself"), Christian Science ("True Blue"), New Age ("Secret"), and Dispensational Premillennialism ("Who's That Girl"). She is an avid supporter of the Kabbalah Centre, whose website promises to teach you how "72 unique combinations of Hebrew letters from Chapter 14 of the book of Exodus create a spiritual vibration that is a powerful antidote to the negative energy of the human ego" if you purchase the associated *Technology for the Soul* book.

Kabbalah forbids masturbation (for the common-sense reason that wasted sperm are abandoned souls that become demons) and woman-on-top sex (based on a bad reaction to a Penelope Cruz movie), and also recommends that the best time for sex is Saturday morning, when you can "distract your children with 'Smurfs' cartoons."

However, everyone knows that the best time for sex is in fact "after prom, in the bathroom of the hotel suite that you and your twelve closest friends rented." And the rest of Kabbalah is a mishmash of New Age ideas and cult-like practices, which are amply debunked elsewhere in the book. Kabbalah is false.

29

JuBu is false

JuBu is a portmanteau of Judaism and Buddhism, formed by taking the worst parts of each. According to a page I found on the internet, approximately one third of American Buddhists are actually JuBus (this was corroborated by a different page on the internet). Celebrities like "Sex and the City" star Sarah Jessica Parker, *Wildcats* coach Goldie Hawn, "Iron Man" Robert Downey Jr., and Beastie Boy "MCA" have all (under harsh interrogation and the threat of waterboarding) admitted to being JuBus. For some reason JuBus are almost always Jews who start dabbling in Buddhism, never the other way around (which is why JuBu is listed in this chapter). Converts typically cite one of several common reasons for converting:

- Jewish laws both insane and onerous; Buddhist rituals merely insane
- To anger parents without getting disinherited (as is common with conversions to Christianity or Islam)
- Obsessed with flax
- Buddhism popular with Allen Ginsburg
- To recapture sense of ecstasy associated with first pair of Manolo Blahniks
- Judaism not mystical enough
- To fill void left by end of "Paul's Boutique" era
- Need ascetic break from fat-fried Jewish dietary staples
- Confusion between "Eight days of Passover" and "Noble Eightfold Path"
- Buddhist teachings about suffering help explain painfully-interminable synagogue services

However, Judaism denies the existence of a cycle of death and re-birth, discourages the weighing of flax, and insists that there is only one noble truth ("I am the LORD!"). Moreover, Buddhism denies the existence of Doctor Goddenstein, mandates the eating of bacon, and encourages intermarriage. Hence Judaism and Buddhism are quite plainly incompatible, and JuBu is false.

RELIGIONS THAT EVERYONE AGREES ARE TYPES OF CHRISTIANITY

30

The story of Jesus

I know what you're thinking: "Oh, great, another person who wants to talk to me about Jesus."

First it was that Christian rock group in high school who played a really terrible cover of "Carry On Wayward Son" in an attempt to "change lives" at the RJHS Battle of the Bands. Then there were the College Crusaders, who used to tackle you on the way to class, sit on your back so you couldn't get up, hold a Bible in your face, and force you to read it. There was the math professor who handed out the Gospel of John on the last day of class, insisting that – unlike the problem sets you'd been handing in all semester – all its answers were "correct."

Also that wears-sweaters-even-in-the-summer girl in the next cubicle at work with a "Footprints" poster on her wall and a cross necklace and a co-ed Bible study she's always trying to bribe you to attend. And finally that politician's autobiography, the one that he signed and gave you a copy of in a transparent attempt to buy your vote, that for its first thirty chapters was a standard tale of crooked game shows and prisoners-of-war and limb-amputation and minor-league baseball and political corruption, but whose last thirty pages unexpectedly sprung an awkward side-of-the-freeway, eyes-full-of-tears, god-speaking-to-my-heart conversion story on you. It's happened to all of us.

So I hope it will relieve you to know that I don't care about your soul (as I feel quite confident that there is no such thing), that the only love I'm trying to spread is my love of fortified wines with unusual flavors like Kiwi-Strawberry and Bling-Bling Blue Raspberry, and that the only thing I'm trying to save is money to pay off my credit-card debt.

Who was Jesus?

Depending on which books you believe, Jesus was either a fictional character, god, the son of god, the messiah prophesied in the Old Testament, a schizophrenic who believed he was the messiah prophesied in the Jewish

Bible, a performance artist who pretended to be the messiah prophesied in the Jewish Bible, a fictional character, the inventor of gunpowder, the true author of Shakespeare's plays, a miracle worker, an alien who came to earth from the planet Ork in an egg-shaped spaceship, a (non-divine) prophet, a Jewish carpenter, Karen Carpenter, a fictional character, or Elvis.

The Gospels

The story of Jesus comes from the four New Testament gospels of Matthew, Mark, Luke, and John, which are (according to Christians) infallible, but which also all contradict each other in a variety of ways:

- Matthew traces Jesus's ancestry back to King David; Luke establishes Jesus as a Kennedy.
- John implies that Jesus was Black; other gospels suggest Latino.
- Jesus came either to "give his life as a ransom for many" (Mark), to "preach the good news of the Kingdom of God" (Luke), so that "those who believed in him would have eternal life" (John), or to "chew gum and kick ass, and he's all out of gum" (Matthew)
- Luke argues that other gospels' Last Supper was actually brunch
- Jesus killed by either the Jews (Mark), the Romans (Matthew), the CIA (with Lee Harvey Oswald as a patsy) (John), or "a broken heart" (Luke)
- Jesus's last words on the cross described as either "My god, why have you forsaken me?" (Matthew), "Forgive them, for they do not know what they are doing!" (Luke), "It is finished!" (John), or "Peter, I can see your house from up here!" (Mark)
- Resurrection of Jesus announced either by angel (Matthew), by two angels (Luke), by young boy (Mark), or by Marv Albert (John)
- Matthew only gospel to suggest "Because he was hung like this" punch-line to theological quandary "Why was Jesus so popular with the ladies?"

In what follows, I have used my unparalleled collection of scholarly abilities to navigate these contradictions and get at the truth of the story, insofar as there is any truth to be found in a collection of overlapping fictional fairy tales.

Around the year 10 B.C., people started to wonder about the C in B.C. and began speculating what calendar-worthy event was only a decade away. Some people thought the Circus was coming to town. Others predicted that Cars were on the verge of being invented. A third group suspected that Chinese Food would soon be introduced to the Middle East, although most everyone else argued that would have been B.C.F. And a small group of Jews decided that the messiah (or Christ) prophesied in the Old Testament book "Isaiah" was on his way.

The virgin birth

Imagine that you're dating this girl who claims to be a virgin. You pressure her, but she won't sleep with you. You play "Theme from Shaft" on your stereo, but still she won't sleep with you. You marry her, and still she won't sleep with you. Suddenly, she gets pregnant. Would you think

(a) My virgin wife was miraculously impregnated by the holy spirit, who is both god and not-god, and will be giving birth to the son of god, who will be the Jewish messiah and will also be both god and not-god, or

(b) My so-called "virgin" wife is actually a cheating slut?

Unless, of course, you are the biggest chump in the world, you would choose the second explanation. But a young Jewess named Mary managed to sell her husband Joseph (Hebrew for "biggest chump in the world") on the first explanation, despite the fact that it was (according to best estimates) only 4 B.C., and therefore that little baby Jesus was in fact several years too early to be the forthcoming C (which, it turned out, was *cheesecake*).

Baptism and temptation

The Isaiah-prophesiers latched onto young Jesus and paid his way through carpentry school. After finishing some kitchen cabinets in southern Israel, he came across NWA Texas Heavyweight Champion John "the Baptist" Zacharias, a renegade Jewish preacher whose finishing move was to push people into the Jordan River. (His gimmick also involved offering to absolve them of their sins afterward.) For reasons that have never become clear, Jesus insisted that John baptize him.

Christians, who believe that Jesus never sinned a day in his life ("he didn't intend to underpay those call girls"), argued for centuries afterward over why Jesus would have needed water-park absolution. Some believed Jesus wanted to set an example for his future followers. Others believed Jesus wanted to be manhandled by a large Jewish wrestler (Goldberg and

Barry Horowitz, of course, both being millennia from being born). And most concluded that Jesus was merely hot and sweaty from doing desert carpentry and just wanted a dip to cool off. Regardless of his motivation, Christians adopted the cool dip baptism as an integral part of their religion, and they have dominated competitive swimming events ever since.

Jesus next went camping in the desert, although he managed not to bring any food or water and had to go without for forty days. Although he went by himself, he was quickly joined by biblical troublemaker Satan, aka The Satan, aka The Fallen Angel, aka the serpent from Eden, aka the Devil, aka Macavity the Mystery Cat, aka Etaoin Shrdlu, aka Azazel, aka Snorlax, aka The Tempter, aka Snake Eyes, aka Ambrose Bierce, aka Beelzebub, aka Professor X, aka Damien, aka Bustopher Jones, aka Jigglypuff, aka the Mull of Kintyre, aka the Wicked One, aka Taco, aka Friend of a Friend of Jerry Garcia, aka Belial, aka Abaddon, aka the fiddle-contest guy, aka Gene Simmons, aka the Anti-Christ, aka Destro, aka Lucifer, aka Geodude, aka Old Scratch, aka The Rum Tum Tugger, aka Mephistopheles, aka Mister Red and Horny, aka Angel of the Bottomless Pit, aka Serpentor, aka Clootie, aka Ebru Labadon, aka The Bride of Beth Chedruharazzeb, aka Prince of Darkness, aka Slippery Pete.

Slippery Pete attempted to get Jesus to use his supernatural powers (in particular, x-ray vision, wall-crawling, and psionic blast) to demonstrate his divine nature, but (probably citing yet another movie quote about faith) Jesus refused and eventually returned home to visit friends and family.

Jesus's ministry

Soon afterward, most likely to escape his creditors, Jesus left his hometown of Nazareth (best known for a power-ballad cover of The Everly Brothers' "Love Hurts"), and moved to the lakeside resort of Capernaum to practice his bass-fishing. It was here that Jesus began his now-famous practice of performing magic tricks ("miracles") to impress the superstitious locals:

- Reduced the fever of a sick woman using only a cold compress
- Caught a bullet in his teeth
- Performed first-ever man-to-pig demon transplant
- Made the Statue of Liberty disappear
- Cursed a fig tree ("your descendants will be baked into Newtons!")
- Created nourishing "stone soup" for starving townspeople
- Walked on water

- Sawed assistant in half
- Raised Lazarus from the dead
- Escaped from straitjacket while suspended from large wooden cross
- Removed then re-attached his thumb
- Survived being buried alive for then-record three days (later surpassed by David Blaine)

In Capernaum Jesus began to recruit apostles from among the local fishermen. He soon became famous for his apocalyptic teachings, for his syndicated advice column "The J-Man's Judicious Jivings," and for the sermons he delivered to large crowds on mountainsides, in plains, and in repurposed basketball arenas. He also expanded his ministry by appealing to those on the margins of society, including prostitutes, comfort-women, eve-teasers, pornographers, stalkers, buggerers, tax-collectors, mail-carriers, bootleggers, rum-runners, human-traffickers, balloon-swallowers, arms-smugglers, ankle-biters, monkey-lickers, mouth-breathers, cattle-humpers, and lawyers. As many of his followers were uneducated, Jesus typically taught using parables, including "The Good Samaritan," "The Ten Virgins," "The Crow and the Pitcher," "The Frog and the Ox," and "The Congressman and the Nubile Intern."

Eventually Jesus brought his followers to the Temple in Jerusalem. In response to being quoted exorbitant transaction fees by the local money-changers, Jesus lost his temper and went on a small-scale rampage, angering local authorities.

The last supper and crucifixion

After organizing the ominously-titled Last Supper and posing for a portrait with his friends, Jesus was arrested by the Roman authorities, who were so inept that (despite Jesus's fame and popularity) they were only able to identify him with the help of his Judas-like friend Judas.

Denied his Constitutionally-guaranteed due process, Jesus was whipped, crucified, thorn-crowned, spear-poked, and mocked until dead. Some of Jesus's friends hauled his body down and told everyone they were going to put it in a tomb. Several days later the tomb was found to be empty, which Jesus's followers chose to take as evidence that he had been resurrected, that they should continue his ministry, and that he had ascended to heaven where he ruled (and continues to rule) alongside his father, who is also him. Jesus occasionally makes reappearances on tortillas, freshly-washed windows, and lasagna-dish grime, but mostly keeps to himself these days.

Christian apologetics

Is there any reason to believe this crazy story is true? Most Christ-believers are content to rely on the expertise of apologetics ("I'm *sorry* my arguments don't make any sense, but have you read the source material?") like science-fiction author and "theologian" C.S. Lewis, who is generally credited with the "Four L's" argument for the divinity of Jesus:

> If Jesus never existed, then he is only a Legend. But the Bible says he exists (and also I saw his face in a tortilla), so that must not be the case. Moreover, if he were a Liar then (not because it is impossible but only because I say so) he would not have been willing to die for his beliefs (which we know he did, because the Bible says so), so that must also not be the case. If he were a Lunatic then (not because it is logically necessary but only because I say so) he would have been put in a straitjacket (which we know he was not, because the Bible doesn't mention it), so that must also not be the case. Therefore, the only option left (not because we have actually excluded all other possibilities beginning with the letter L, since in fact Jesus might be a Leprechaun or a Ladybug or a Lunchbox, but only because I say so) is that he is/was Lord.

If this argument seems convincing to you, Lewis has written a whole series of similarly-compelling children's books, about lions (who represent Jesus), witches (who represent the gold standard), and wardrobes (which represent Scandinavian self-assembly-furniture warehouses). In any event, it's worth investigating the various claims of the Jesus-worshippers.

Christianity is false

Christianity: The belief that a cosmic Jewish Zombie who was his own father can make you live forever if you symbolically eat his flesh and telepathically tell him you accept him as your master, so he can remove an evil force from your soul that is present in humanity because a rib-woman was convinced by a talking snake to eat from a magical tree.

– found on the internet

Considering how widespread Christianity is, its theology is surprisingly complicated and outlandish. It starts with Adam and Eve, the first humans, who were created by god in the paradise of Eden, a volcano in Auckland, New Zealand. Tired of being shot down by the ladies as "too benevolent," god planted a Tree of Knowledge (i.e. sex) and a Tree of Life (i.e. sex), both of whose fruit he deemed off-limits for eating. As there were in those days no laws against entrapment, he then allowed the snakey Satan into Eden, to tempt Adam and Eve into eating the forbidden fruit of knowledge and (hence) committing the forbidden act of "education."

Original sin

This transgression, commonly referred to as "The Fall of Man" but also known as "Two Bad Apples" and "Rubik's Magic Snake," gave god the excuse he needed to expel Adam and Eve from paradise. Furthermore, on account of Eve's "Original Sin," all subsequent human beings were born covered in a sticky layer of sin whose presence allowed god to consign them to an infinitely unpleasant afterlife of torture in hell, the domain ruled by god's snakey conspirator.

(If you have not been indoctrinated from birth with the notion of Original Sin, you may find the idea of punishing people for their distant ancestors' wrongdoings a little bit distasteful. If you point this out to Christians, they will patiently explain that your sense of taste is wrong, possibly as a result of Satan's influence.)

For thousands of years, the story goes, god was content to let people suffer eternal damnation, until one day he didn't have any condoms, magically impregnated Mary with himself, and became (also) the baby Jesus. By dying on the cross (but not really, since god is immortal and is supposed to have come back to life three days later), god/Jesus performed "the ultimate sacrifice," opening an avenue to salvation, a process that allows the dead to spend their eternities in heaven rather than in hell.

Sign-wielding idiots

Possibly if you have attended a sporting event (or watched one on TV) you have seen an idiot holding a large sign reading "JOHN 3:16." Contrary to what you might first think, this sign-wielding moron is neither quoting gambling odds nor proposing a mid-afternoon gay tryst in the restroom. Instead he is referencing and attempting to get you to look up a Bible verse:

> For God so loved the world that he gave his one and only Son, that whoever believes in him shall not perish but have eternal life.

According to this line of thinking, if you believe in Jesus (or god, depending on how you interpret the dangling pronoun) then you will become "saved" and receive "eternal life." This assertion of belief most commonly consists of a blubbering cry-storm in front of a church congregation, a manhandling in the mosh-pit at a Stryper concert, or an any-port-in-a-storm deathbed prayer.

This line of thinking, of course, neglects to mention that god (being both all-powerful and smooth with the ladies) could have another son anytime he wanted to, and also that god is the one who took away eternal life in the first place. It also glosses over "JOHN 3:18," which actually is a gay restroom tryst, and which also claims that it is already too late to start believing in Jesus:

> Whoever believes in him is not condemned, but whoever does not believe stands condemned already because he has not believed in the name of God's one and only Son.

Many Christians maintain that an authentic demonstration of belief also requires a John-Zacharias-style baptism, while many others insist that it demands ritual pseudo-cannibalism involving holy wine and crackers that are magically and tastelessly and imperceptibly converted into the actual blood and flesh of Jesus mid-swig and mid-chew.

Trinitarianism

Additionally, most Christians believe that god is actually a "trinity" of three distinct persons combined into one "godhead" through "perichoresis" (which I'm pretty sure is some kind of gum disease):

god the father: Also known as Don Vito Corleone, god the father rules a terrifying crime organization, yet is unable to refuse requests made on his daughter's wedding day. Whenever he sees orange, it means that someone is going to die.

god the son: Jesus is both god and the son of god, which (according to my calculations) means that he impregnated his mother, which is more than just a little bit gross.

god the holy spirit: He will come in one of the pre-chosen forms. During the rectification of the Vuldronaii, he came as a large and moving Torb. Then, during the third reconciliation of the last of the Meketrex Supplicants, they chose a new form for him – that of a Giant Sloar! Many Shubs and Zuuls knew what it was to be roasted in the depths of the Sloar that day I can tell you!

They are quick to admit that this point of view makes no logical sense, usually arguing that "god doesn't have to make logical sense." Alternatively, they might offer the uncompelling analogy that an egg is three distinct persons (a yolk, a white, and a shell) combined in one "egghead," ignoring the fact that the shell never claimed to be the yolk's father and yet also a yolk, and also the fact that the white has never been claimed to dwell inside people who believe in eggs.

Prayer

Jesus taught that prayer should be a private affair:

> And when you pray, do not be like the hypocrites, for they love to pray standing in the synagogues and on the street corners to be seen by men. I tell you the truth, they have received their reward in full. But when you pray, go into

your room, close the door and pray to your Father, who is
unseen. Then your Father, who sees what is done in secret,
will reward you.

Matthew 6:5-6

Despite this (obvious) proscription, Christians gather together in
churches to worship on holidays like Christmas (a pagan festival cannily
repackaged as Jesus's birthday), Easter (a Jewish festival cannily repackaged
as Jesus's re-birthday), Saint Patrick's Day (an Irish festival cannily repackaged as Jesus's green-beer-drinking day), and Saint Groundhog's Day (a
Bill Murray movie cannily repackaged as Jesus's weather-forecasting day).
More-devoted Christians attend weekly church services on Sunday mornings, or simply sit in front of the television and watch others attending
these services (I assume, since there's no other explanation for the sheer
volume of such programs).

Jesus the Jew

Although Jesus was himself a Jew, he taught that his followers no longer
needed to obey Jewish law:

> Do not think that I have come to abolish the Law or the
> Prophets; I have not come to abolish them but to fulfill them.
> I tell you the truth, until heaven and earth disappear, not the
> smallest letter, not the least stroke of a pen, will by any means
> disappear from the Law until everything is accomplished.

Matthew 5:17-18

OK, so maybe he didn't "teach" it per se, but it's certainly what
he would have wanted, at least according to the crab fisherman and tax
collectors and zealots who continued his ministry, and who noticed
shortly after his death that fear of circumcision (and, to a lesser degree,
love of bacon) was costing them converts and causing them not to make
quota. Based on these and other (contradictory) quotes, Christians tend
to ignore Old Testament teachings they find burdensome (e.g. dietary
laws) while enthusiastically supporting others that strike their fancy (e.g.
gay-stoning).

At this point the various flavors of Christianity diverge, offering
widely varied opinions on everything from "should our priests be allowed
to have sex?" to "should our priests be allowed to have gay sex?" to

"should our priests be allowed to have gay sex with minors?" to "should our priests be allowed to have gay sex with minors in the confession booth after boys choir practice?" to "should we ship our priests who were caught having gay sex with minors in the confession booth after boys choir practice off to Jemez Springs before they get prosecuted and we get sued?" The further details of just how Christianity is false, then, will have to be examined flavor by flavor.

32

Catholicism is false

If you like your Christianity old-school, Catholicism is the faith for you. The Catholic Church considers itself the original form of Christianity, virtually unchanged from Jesus's day (except that over the years it has become wealthy and powerful enough to establish a fancy web site at www.va where the faithful can play slick online games like *Vatican Tower Defense* and *Communion Mania* and *Indulgence Wars* and *Bejeweled*). To distinguish itself from the more recent Christian denominations, Catholicism brags that it embodies "the four marks of the true church":

one: the church does not tolerate dissent

holy: the church leaks water

catholic: the church never changes, not even when science provides sensible explanations of its mysteries

apostolic: the church's chain of weirdo leaders traces itself all the way back to Jesus

Priests and popes

The Catholic church operates in a strict hierarchy. Churches are run by priests, who report to arch-priests, who report to pre-adjutor bishops, who report to co-adjutor bishops, who report to bishops, who report to metropolitans, who report to cardinals, who report to patriarchs, who report to the Pope, who reports to god. This middle-management-heavy structure has made the church somewhat sclerotic (hence its nickname "an unholy blend of Monty Python and Big Brother"), and has left it beholden to the preachers unions, who have enough clout to insist that criminally-pedophile priests be given cushy administrative jobs rather than fired.

Catholics consider the Pope to be the spiritual successor of Peter, who tended to forget his own name, and whom Jesus tasked with building his church:

And I tell you that you are Peter, and on this rock I will build my church, and the gates of Hell will not overcome it.

Matthew 16:18

Peter's successors were only marginally successful until the fourth century, when the Roman emperor Constantine converted to Christianity and established it as the official religion of his empire. The papacy gained additional prestige with the advent of papal infallibility, the idea that whenever a pope asserts one of his teachings as a "solemn papal definition," the teaching is assured of being correct. The only limit on this power is that pope cannot infallibly contradict a previous infallible teaching, as this would cause the universe to explode.

Popes are elected by their peers and serve until they die, are killed, or are impeached. The Pope carries a number of honorary titles, including "Bishop of Rome," "Vicar of Christ," "Der Popemeister," "Servant of the Servants of the Servants of God," and "Most Valuable Primate." He lives in (and rules) the Vatican City, an independent country located within Rome, where Latin is the official language, "Onward Singapore" is the national motto, and Blood of Christ is the national drink. He also drives around in a special "Popemobile," throws curved "Poperangs" at his enemies, uses a "Popecave" as his secret hideout, and carries a "Shark Repellent Pope Spray" to get himself out of squaline jams.

Sacraments

Catholics believe that they must participate in seven sacraments (so called because they first became popular in Sacramento, California):

Baptism: taking a bath with a priest

Confirmation: being anointed with Christ's sacred jism (often called "Chrism" so it sounds less gross)

Eucharist: eating crackers and drinking wine while a priest magically transforms them into Jesus's flesh and blood

Penance: confessing your crimes to an anonymous priest in a darkened booth while he fondles himself (alternatively, while you fondle yourself)

Anointing of the Sick: recently rebranded as "X-treme Unction!" to sound edgier

Holy Orders: "the co-adjutor bishop would like a double-double 'animal-style', fries 'well-done', and a Neapolitan shake"

Matrimony: a special Catholic form of marriage in which divorce is absolutely prohibited, although wealthy couples can often use money to persuade priests to completely annul the marriage and pretend like it never happened, especially when the marriage suffers from a fatal flaw such as "undispensed lack of form"

According to the Church, these sacraments are "efficacious signs of grace, instituted by Christ and entrusted to the Church, by which divine life is dispensed to us." As I suspect this definition makes as little sense to you as it does to me, I researched "divine life" and discovered that it is some sort of Hindu cult founded by Paramapujya Gurudev Sri Swami Sivanandaji Maharaj in the 1930's. The popular Catholic web sites are all strangely silent on why Catholics would want to participate in a Hindu cult, making me suspect that it has something to do with "curry envy."

Celibacy

Starting with the fourth-century Synod of Elvira (motto: "Giddy Up Oom Poppa Oom Poppa Mow Mow"), it became official church policy that priests (and therefore Popes) remain celibate, leading to an utterly-predictable drop-off in the popularity of priesthood as a career that continues to this day.

Now, when you put sexually-frustrated old men in candle-lit confessional booths with nubile young boys, ugly things happen, which has led to a number of high-profile abuse cases levied against the church. Commentators have proposed a number of explanations:

- Satan
- True identity of Catholic Church as "Whore of Babylon"
- Negligence on the part of seminary-admissions-office gay-screeners
- Lax standards toward boy-touching resulting from Second Vatican Council
- Celibacy unreasonable thing to expect of grown men
- Wicked altar boys "led them on"

Accused priests have typically been moved to different parishes and (in instances of extreme recidivism) occasionally fired and prosecuted. Many Catholic churches have also been forced to pay out large cash settlements, which they usually attempt to recoup by agitating for relaxed immigration standards for people coming from countries with large populations of poorly-educated, highly-credulous, heavily-tithing Catholics.

Saints

Catholics also place great importance on saints, exceptionally holy people who have died and can be demonstrated to have performed at least two miracles. Many of them are designated as patrons of specific professions or hobbies, whose practitioners feel a special kinship with and offer prayers to them. For example, St. Anger is the patron saint of internet-hating heavy metal bands, and St. Drogo is the patron saint of unattractive people, baristas, unattractive baristas, people with hernias, sheep, sheep with hernias, and the mentally ill. While all saints are important, the following are probably the most important:

Archie Manning: had worst record in NFL history among quarterbacks with at least 100 starts
Arnold: encouraged peasants to drink beer rather than water; patron saint of fratboys
Barbara: executed by her pagan father for converting to Christianity; killed him with lightning from beyond the grave
Cyprian: as a pagan magician, summoned demons to rape a Christian virgin; when unsuccessful, converted to Christianity himself
Elsewhere: stellar ensemble cast included Denzel Washington, Helen Hunt, Mark Harmon, and Ed Begley, Jr.
Fiacre: legendarily afraid of girls; patron saint of eHarmony.com
Giuseppi of Cupertino: not very bright; able to levitate
Hubbins: patron saint of quality footwear
Justina: as a virgin, was almost raped by pagan-summoned demons; patron saint of women who were almost raped by demons
Petersburg: also known as Leningrad

At this point you are probably wondering how you can become a saint yourself. To help you out, I have put together the following five-step program:

1. Become a Catholic. (If you are already Catholic, you may skip this step.)
2. Kiss up to the Pope. (I hear he likes World War II memorabilia.)
3. Die. (If you can manage to die as a martyr, even better.)
4. Perform a miracle. (Curing a non-fatal illness is a good choice.)
5. Perform another miracle. (Making the sun dance around the sky is recommended, although turning wine into Jesus's blood could work in a pinch.)

If you try this, I'd love to hear how it works out for you. Drop me a note: your.religion.is.false@gmail.com

Sex

The Catholic Church has extreme views on sex, arguing that it is permissible only between married couples, and only for the purposes of procreation and (occasionally) revenge. Accordingly, Catholics are prohibited from using condoms (even in Swaziland), from getting lap dances or table dances (even at Captain Creams), from commissioning Mother-Teresa-simulacrum RealDolls, and from mentally undressing priests.

In addition, Catholics are adamantly opposed to abortion, even in the case of tentacle rape, arguing that life begins at the instant of conception, and that an eight-cell, half-tentacle zygote has just the same "right to life" as you do. (If you point out that some huge proportion of conceptions end in spontaneous abortion, Catholics will usually either blame this on Satan, argue that abortion is actually acceptable "when god does it," or pretend that they only understand Latin.)

Super Mariology

Catholics have a special reverence for the Virgin Mary, as the Bible specifically commands them:

> But when the time had fully come, God sent his Son, born of a woman, born under law
>
> Galatians 4:4

Don't feel bad if you can't figure out how this verse demands that you revere Mary. The Catholic Church itself took 400 years to decide that this passage required special Marian devotion. But ever since, Catholics have created all sorts of tacky Marian art, including statues, candles, velvet paintings, snow globes, mobiles, collages, mosaics, and YouTube videos.

Furthermore, many Catholics around the world have discovered vaguely Mary-shaped patterns and burn marks on tortillas, windows, toast, underpasses, and underwear. Other Catholics will eagerly flock (and pay) to see these miracles.

Apart from her well-known roles as virgin and mom and skid mark, Mary also serves as "Mediatrix" (an ombudsperson for souls stuck in Purgatory, the waiting-area for heaven), "Co-Redemptrix" (someone possessing a unique spiritual union with Jesus on account of having passed him through her vagina), and "Bellatrix" (a pure-blood witch who tortured aurors Alice and Frank Longbottom to the point of insanity). As a result,

Catholics like to offer prayers to Mary. The following is a pretty typical example:

> This girl Mary I knew so well
> She stayed in a stable, not no motel
> Nazareth, that's where she dwelled
> "Get your butt home Jesus!" she used to yell
> She shampooed every night with Prell
> It gave her hair that classy smell
> She picked me up whenever I fell
> I knew Mary well cause she saved me from hell
>
> Mary, Mary, why ya buggin?
> Just like Jesus, you keep on chuggin'!

Other well-known Marian prayers include "Along Comes Mary," "There's Something About Mary," "Proud Mary," and "Mary, Mary, Quite Contrary" (but not the Andrew Dice Clay version, which apparently hits a little bit too close to home).

Catholic festivals

Besides the usual Christian holidays, Catholics have a variety of day-of-week-specific festivals, including Manic Monday (when you have to catch an early train just to be at work by nine), Fat Tuesday (a Mardi-Gras-like party where drunk girls flash strangers in exchange for plastic beads), Ash Wednesday (the beginning of Lent, a forty-day pre-Easter fast), Monday Thursday (a celebration of the betrayal of Jesus by Judas), Freaky Friday (commemorating the time that Jodie Foster switched bodies with her mother), Holy Saturday (celebrating the misplacement of Christ's crucified corpse), and Palm Sunday (the anniversary of an occasion when Jesus is supposed to have ridden two donkeys).

The Da Vinci Code

During his lifetime, Jesus hung out with a prostitute named Mary Magdalene. While most Christians believe that their relationship was nothing more than exorcist-exorcee, a few maintain that they got married and had children together (probably with trendy names like Kiara, Kylee, or Peyton). And while most Christians believe that the Holy Grail merely refers to the cup that Jesus drank from at his last supper that is now hidden in the Canyon of the Crescent Moon and that gives eternal life to anyone who drinks from it, a few insist that it actually refers to the Sacred Feminine, who carried on the bloodline of Christ (through Peyton).

Catholic groups like the Priory of Sion (a secret orgy society) and Opus Dei (a ministry of celibate ex-con albinos who live in communal housing) have over the years been locked in a murderous struggle over this grail secret. Sadly, no one outside the church really cares what the grail represents; we just want to see Tom Hanks and Audrey Tatou get it on.

The Cadaver Synod

No discussion of Catholicism would be complete without mentioning the Cadaver Synod, which (contrary to popular belief) is neither a *Star Wars* villain nor a character from *Mortal Kombat*. In 897, Pope Stephen VI (or VII, depending on whether you count the Stephen who died after being elected Pope but before being sworn in as Pope as a Pope) dug up the corpse of his predecessor Formosus, seated him on a throne, and "prosecuted" him for a variety of only-interesting-to-Catholicism-nerds crimes.

Although Formosus's corpse refused to incriminate himself, he was found guilty, defingered, buried, unburied, weighted, and thrown in a river. The public, disgusted with Stephen's antics, fished out Formosus's corpse again, attributed to it a variety of miracles, and strangled Stephen.

The Catholic Church has never been as cool since. Not that it matters, since no one is infallible, pretending that your marriage never happened is dishonest and demeaning, and dead people (like alive people) cannot perform miracles. Catholicism is false.

33

Orthodoxy is false

Like Catholicism, Orthodox Christianity also claims to be the true church descended from Jesus's ministry. Indeed, for many centuries both were the same church. But over the years the Western church (represented by the Bishop of Rome) and the Eastern church (represented by the Patriarch of Constantinople) repeatedly tangled over a number of crucial doctrinal questions at intermittent ecumenical councils. The first seven (which all took place pre-schism) should give you a good idea of their scope:

Nicaea 325: "Was Jesus made from the same ectoplasm as god, or from merely similar ectoplasm?"

Constantinople 381: "Is god three things, one thing, or three things and one thing (which, according to my math, equals four things)?"

Ephesus 431: "Should the pope start wearing a funny hat?"

Chalcedon 451: "Should Euthychianism be feared as a form of Docetism, or is it an appropriate response to the threat of Nestorianism?" [Enraged at the outcome, the Church of Alexandria broke off on its own shortly afterward.]

Constantinople 553: "Can we finally put this Nestorianism issue to rest, please?"

Constantinople 680: "Does Jesus have one will or two wills, and if he has two wills how do we decide who inherits his Camaro?"

Nicaea 787: "Should we look at pictures of naked ladies when we pray?"

To modern believers, who have more exciting things to worry about like "On a scale of 1 to 10, how much does god hate fags?" and "At what trimester does abortion become a sin?" and "Why is the priest touching me like that?" these hardly seem like topics worth getting worked up about. However, life in the first millennium was so boring that obscure theological arguments were a primary source of entertainment.

The East-West Schism

After holding separate Eighth Councils in the late 800s, the Catholic and Orthodox churches finally reached the breaking point in 1054, when the East-West Schism led to a complete separation of the churches. Prominent players in this feud included Suge Knight and Tupac (whose "Wonder Why They Call U A Bitch" represented the West), and Biggie Smalls (whose "What's Beef?" did the same for the East).

Despite the schism, the practice of Orthodoxy is not substantially different from the practice of Catholicism. Orthodox priests, unlike Catholic priests, are allowed to have sex; and Orthodox churches, unlike Catholic churches, are typically topped with pungent, onion-shaped domes. Orthodoxy would probably be more popular if not for its bizarre insistence on conducting its masses in ugly-sounding languages like Moldovan and Bulgarian and Bessarabian.

Today Orthodox Christians are best known for their annual "Greek Festivals," where they open the doors of their churches to non-believers, break plates, sell *loukoumathes*, perform festive Greek dances, play *bouzouki* music, and shout "Opa!" But no matter how tasty feta cheese is, Orthodoxy is just as false as its near-identical cousin Catholicism.

34

Conservative Protestantism is false

In the year 1517, a German priest named Martin Luther (unrelated to the similarly-named king and civil rights activist) grew frustrated with the rampant commercialism (and high prices) surrounding indulgences, sin-forgivenesses sold by the Catholic Church. He summarized his displeasure in "Ninety-Five Theses" and tacked them to the door of a church in Wittenberg.

Despite pressure from the Pope (who attempted to force him to eat a "diet of worms" as punishment), Luther refused to recant his theses and was excommunicated in 1521. He proceeded to violate a number of Catholic rules, including clerical celibacy (when he got married), biblical non-translation (when he translated the Bible), congregational non-singing (when he introduced congregational singing), and pro-semitism (when he propounded anti-semitism).

The Lutheran Church grew out of his protests, and was quickly followed by many other types of Protestants, including Calvinists, Methodists, African Methodists, Stanislavski Methodists, Puritans, Impuritans, Presbyterians, Free Presbyterians, Pay Presbyterians, Zwinglians, Congregationalists, Anti-Congregationalists, Semi-Congregationalists, Wesleyans, Nazarenes, Restorationists, De-Restorationists, Waldensians, Civil-Disobedians, Reformeds, Evangelicals, Huguenots, Baptists, Regular Baptists, Constipated Baptists, Churches of God, Churches without God, Salvation Army, Salvation Coast Guard, and Huguenots.

Around the same time, British king Henry VIII wanted to divorce his wife Catherine of Aragon, who had failed to provide him a male heir, and who also tended to hog the covers. When the Pope (who, inconveniently, was being held prisoner by Catherine's nephew) refused to grant the annulment, Henry broke with Rome and appointed himself head of the Church of England, forming the (eventually Protestant) denomination of Anglicanism, which later spawned Episcopalianism as well.

There are many differences between the Protestant denominations, but they are all supremely boring and have very little to do with why Protestantism is false. For instance, the Lutheran Church Missouri Synod and the Wisconsin Evangelical Lutheran Synod disagree primarily on the questions of whether Sunday-school teachers are "divinely inspired," whether women should be allowed to vote in primary elections, and whether "the only ship worth a damn" is fellowship or friendship. (In fact, the only ship worth a damn is Jefferson Starship.) Accordingly, our time is better spent focusing on the similarities.

Principles of Protestantism

Conservative Protestants strictly follow three universal principles, all of which revolve around the idea of "I'm sick of the Pope telling me what to do":

1. "If the Bible says it, I believe it. If the Bible doesn't say it, I don't believe it. If the Pope says it, for sure I don't believe it, unless the Bible says it too, in which case I have to ask the pastor on a call-in AM radio show what I think."

2. "It doesn't matter how good or evil the Pope thinks you are. If you accept Jesus as your 'savior', you're going to heaven, and if you don't, you're going to hell."

3. "I'm sick of the Pope telling me what to do."

The first causes all sorts of problems, as it forces conservative Protestants to believe that the world is only 6000 years old, to disbelieve in all sorts of useful science, to insist that one man both built a boat capable of carrying and subsequently collected two members of every species on earth (including, apparently, all five-million-plus species of beetles), and to assert that π equals exactly 3. The second causes all sorts of problems, as it has allowed a number of Nixon-era criminals to establish lucrative post-incarceration prison ministries. The third is actually an exceptionally sensible position, in a stopped-clock-is-right-twice-a-day kind of way (although Protestants typically justify it on the grounds that the Catholic Church is the *Revelation*-prophesied "Whore of Babylon," when in fact everyone knows that the Whore of Babylon is actually the United States of America, who will someday be destroyed by the "beast with seven heads and ten horns," which everyone knows is actually the United Nations).

Protestant practices

There are as many Protestant practices as there are Protestants. Some Protestants (e.g. Baptists) believe that dancing is sinful, while others (e.g. Baptists) believe that drinking alcohol is sinful, and yet others (e.g. Baptists) believe that one should not let oneself be controlled by anything other than god the holy spirit.

Protestants also hold a wide variety of opinions on whether Eucharist crackers and wine are actually transformed into the flesh and blood of Christ, whether they are merely *symbols* of the flesh and blood of Christ, or whether they are just supposed to *taste like* the flesh and blood of Christ (whose flesh and blood, according to legend, actually did taste like crackers and wine).

Conservative Protestants share with Catholics an extreme hatred of both homosexuality and abortion. Accordingly, they tend to send their gay children off to "conversion therapy" (involving techniques ranging from clitoridectomy to shame) and their pregnant children off to single-sex maternity homes (which are full of all sorts of oddly-titillating preggo-on-preggo action, according to the videos on a website I accidentally stumbled across several times).

However, the actual problems with the Catholic Church have less to do with the Pope than they do with its belief in god and Jesus and heaven and hell and miracles and the Bible. As Protestantism doesn't protest any of those, it is quite plainly false.

35

Liberal Protestantism is false

The more liberal forms of Protestantism typically don't get so hung up on the rules of Christianity and are willing to accept that maybe Jesus wasn't the son of god. They usually instead worship Jesus as "a great moral teacher," mostly on the basis of the following precepts:

- If someone hits you, let him hit you again. (Matthew 5:38-39)
- If your right hand causes you to sin, cut it off. (Matthew 5:28-30)
- Looking with lust at a woman makes you guilty of adultery. (Matthew 5:27-28)
- Lend to your enemies, and don't expect them to pay you back (Luke 6:35)
- Give to everyone who asks you, and if someone takes something from you don't ask for it back (Luke 6:30)
- Sell everything you have, and give to the poor (Mark 6:21)
- Hate both your family and yourself (Luke 14:26)

Due to their focuses on universal themes like self-amputation, masochism, self-destructive hyper-generosity, self-loathing, and familial discord, these liberal Christianities have become quite popular.

Ultra-liberal Protestantism

Some ultra-liberal Christians will forgo even these teachings, insisting that the entirety of Jesus's message can be summed up as "be nice to cats" or "put the toilet seat down when you're done using it" or "murder-for-hire is wrong." Many of them insist that Jesus is god (or the son of god, or both) merely because of the power of his anti-hit-man, SPCA-friendly message. (Strangely, few of them take the logical next step of worshipping Bob Barker.)

Some of the more liberal Christians will also argue that Jesus's resurrection was actually a *Weekend at Bernie's*-like slapstick comedy, that all people go to heaven when they die (and that therefore it doesn't really matter whether you believe in their theology or whether you try to lead a virtuous life), and that the reason Mary was a virgin is because Joseph was gay.

Liberal Protestant practices

While most Christians use their churches as meeting places for prayer and worship, liberal Protestants are more likely to use them for Bingo, potlucks, potlatches, covered-dish dinners, faith suppers, Jacob's joins, hot chocolate parties, bring-a-plates, fuddles, and letting homeless junkies sleep in the gym.

Liberal Protestants also often focus on apocryphal stories about the accomplishments of Jesus that are not generally accepted by other Christians:

1. Encouraged grassroots democracy
2. Spoke out against racism, classism, ageism, cripplism, retardism, and mopery
3. Taught "if it's yellow, let it mellow" as part of his "Sermon on the Pot"
4. Fought for nuclear disarmament, and voted against war in Iraq
5. Excoriated economic institutions designed "for the benefit of the few"
6. Supported small farmers by advocating the use of local currencies like Nazareth Dollars
7. Was a feminist (and proud)
8. Sought to mend affirmative action, but not to end it
9. Thought globally, but acted locally
10. Supported underdog Palestinians in conflict with Israelis

Even these non-supernatural teachings of Jesus are pretty poor advice, which means that liberal Protestantism is false.

36

Dispensational Premillenialism is false

Christians believe that at some point Jesus will return to earth, as prophesied in the Bible:

> For the Lord himself will come down from heaven, with a loud command, with the voice of the archangel and with the trumpet call of God, and the dead in Christ will rise first. After that, we who are still alive and are left will be caught up together with them in the clouds to meet the Lord in the air. And so we will be with the Lord forever.

1 Thessalonians 16-17

While most Christians expect that he will simply show up and grab a brewski and start hanging out, a smaller number of Dispensational Premillenialists imagine that his arrival will be preceded by The Rapture, an event in which authentic Christians are vanished directly into heaven, while their clothes and in-flight airplanes and non-believing friends are "Left Behind" to clean up the mess. (Exactly what "authenticity" entails in this context depends on the specific sect of nuts explaining this to you, but always seems to include Scientologist Mimi Rogers.)

Around the same time (these believers believe), the charismatic Nicolae Carpathia will ascend to the Presidency of Romania, soon gaining a promotion to Secretary General of the United Nations. A small "Tribulation Force" of post-Rapture Christian converts, including journalist Cameron "Buck" Williams, airline pilot Rayford Steele, and scientist Chaim Rosenzweig, will oppose and eventually murder Carpathia. However, Carpathia's body will soon thereafter be indwelt by Satan, who will proclaim himself a god and force everyone to worship him. At long last, Jesus will return, defeat Carpathia, and dunk him eternally into a Lake of Fire.

After this defeat, Jesus and the rest of the raptured will reign for 1,000 years, during which time they will re-institute Old Testament practices like animal sacrifice and gay-stoning and slavery. Finally they will hold a Siskel-and-Ebert-style Last Judgment, and only those receiving "two thumbs up" will be taken to heaven.

Kirk Cameron

The most famous Rapture-believer is probably Kirk Cameron, who has spent the majority of his post-"Growing Pains" career debating the theory of evolution on ABC's "Nightline" and posting videos to the internet of himself accosting people on the street and accusing them of not following the Ten Commandments. A typical confrontation looks kind of like the following:

```
Kirk Cameron: Can I ask you a few questions?
Some Guy: Hey, aren't you Kirk Cameron?
KC: I used to be.
SG: Sure, fire away.
KC: Are you a good person?
SG: I think so.
KC: Do you know the Ten Commandments?
SG: You mean, the movie starring Charlton Heston that
    was the last film ever directed by Cecil B.
    DeMille and that won the Academy Award for Best
    Special Effects?
KC: No, I mean the commandments.
SG: I think I know them.
KC: Well, have you ever made an idol?
SG: I voted for Sanjaya on ''American Idol.''
KC: Have you ever coveted your neighbor's house?
SG: I coveted his windows once.  They're double-hung.
KC: And do you always honor your parents?
SG: Well, when I was thirteen, I forgot their
    anniversary.
KC: So, by your own admission, you're an idolator, a
    coveter, and a parent-dishonorer.  If god judges
    you by that standard, do you think you're going
    to heaven or hell?
SG: Hey, what's Joanna Kerns really like?
```

If you decide to hunt these videos down, my favorites are "Kirk ministers to the guy selling *The Homeless Times*," "Kirk ministers to Eric 'Butterbean' Esch," and "Kirk ministers to Alan Thicke." Alas, no matter how "dreamy" Kirk might be, there's not going to be a Rapture, and so Dispensational Premillennialism is false.

37

Snake-handling is false

Of all the chapters in the book, this was probably the saddest to write. For if ever there were a religion you wish were true, it's snake-handling (unless maybe it's Dungeons and Dragons). Whether they're fighting Samuel L. Jackson on a plane, frightening Indiana Jones, acting as familiar for a witch or warlock, or wrapped around a stripper, snakes are awesome, poisonous ones even more so. What little kid hasn't spent blissful days in the woods behind Tony Berger's house, wading in the creek and leaping from rock to rock and shooting at Water Moccasins and Copperheads with Steven Ferris's pellet gun? What teenager hasn't snuck a gourd full of pebbles along on the every-September camping trip to Pine Mountain, crept behind Keith's tent in the middle of the night, and feigned a hilarious fake rattlesnake attack? What adult hasn't adopted a pet python (named Banana) in order to impress women, only to go away to Vegas for a weekend without remembering to turn on the heat lamp, then returning to find Banana curled up in the corner of his tank, frozen to death? Stories like these make me think there must be something universal about snake-fascination.

Snakes and the Bible

Somehow it fell to a handful of Appalachian hillbillies to take that next step of fully integrating snakes into their religion. As is so often the case, it started with the New Testament:

> And these signs shall follow them that believe; In my name shall they cast out devils; they shall speak with new tongues; they shall take up serpents; and if they drink any deadly thing, it shall not hurt them; they shall lay hands on the sick, and they shall recover.

> Mark 16:17-18

You will notice that there are a number of things mentioned in these verses. But by the time George Went Hensley split off from the Church of God in the 1920's, exorcisms had already been called by the Catholics, deadly-thing-drinking by the Heaven's Gate cult, and laying-hands-on by the Christian Scientists. Furthermore, bionic tongue technology was only just invented in 2002. What was left for these redneck Pentecostals but serpents?

(Since then all sorts of patents have expired, and these days the snake-handlers are just as apt to faith-heal and drink poison and speak in nonsense languages as they are to pass a cobra around the church. Nonetheless, snakes remain at the core of their religion.)

As most snake-handlers live in mountainous Kentucky ghost towns that are reachable only by mule, their religion remains largely misunderstood by the rest of the world.

Myths and facts

Myth: Snake-handling is a mandatory part of the religion.

Fact: Those who have lost two or more limbs from snakebites can opt out of further handling (though many choose not to!).

Myth: Snake-handlers believe that god will prevent them from being bitten.

Fact: Snake-handlers believe that the snake will bite them if god so wills, but with the closing of the coal mines, they have so little to live for that they simply don't care.

Myth: "Mixed Nuts" prank spring snakes were invented by George Went Hensley as a religious toy for children.

Fact: "Mixed Nuts" prank spring snakes were invented by Abraham Lincoln to help the North win the Civil War.

Myth: The movie *Snakes on a Plane* was thinly disguised pro-snake-handling propaganda

Fact: The movie *Anaconda* was thinly disguised pro-snake-handling propaganda

Myth: Saint Patrick drove the snakes out of Ireland to thwart the growing influence of the snake-handlers.

Fact: Saint Patrick drove the snakes out of Ireland because he was drunk on green beer.

Myth: "G.I. Joe" villain Serpentor was a snake-handler

Fact: Serpentor was actually a Christian Scientist

Despite great advances in antivenin technology, there are fewer than 40 snake-handling churches remaining today, largely because the religious use of poisonous snakes has been outlawed in most states that are not West Virginia. Given that snake-handlers are routinely killed during their religious services, snake-handling is clearly false.

38

"Cool" Christianity is false

In order to evangelize both to disaffected Christians and to disinterested nonbelievers, many religious groups have attempted to syncretize their faith with various elements of pop culture. These "cool" ministries usually have younger pastors who prefer t-shirts and jeans to comical religious outfits, incessantly restyle their facial hair to match "how the kids are wearing it," insist on being called by their first names (e.g. "Pastor Jim"), play basketball with their congregations (calling fouls based on biblical rules), and blog regularly.

Such ministries include Christian stand-up comedy ("The Clerical Collar Comedy Tour"), Christian musclemen (who, using only anabolic steroids and the power of Jesus, are able to break concrete blocks, lift enormous stones and throw them at heathens, and inflate hot water bottles until they explode), fashion-magazine-themed Bibles ("SEX TIPS OF THE PROPHETS: 10 Tricks That Will Raise the Dead"), t-shirts sloppily parodying once-popular-but-now-forgotten ad campaigns of previous decades ("FORGIVENGRÜVEN"), and Christian-themed popular music.

Christian music

Christian musicians have over the years infiltrated a huge variety of musical genres and infused them with religious lyrics, messages, and horribly-punnish band names. In case you feel the need to start a Christian band yourself, I have prepared for you a list of suggested names, based on your preferred musical genre:

rap: Lord Jeezy
gay heavy metal: For His Glory Hole
British invasion: Simon and the Apostles
disco: Holy Land Vocal Band
punk: Richard Heaven
Motown: The Immaculettes
boy band: 'N Christ

narcocorrido: Los Mesías del Norte
swing: Jericho Droppin' Daddies
shirtless chick pop: Amy Grant
prog rock: Leviticus
new wave: Frankie Goes to Bethlehem
nu metal: Kid Peter
emo: Jesus is the Reason
grunge: Prayer Jam
soft rock: The Jewish Carpenters
twee pop: Andronicus & Junia
techno: Christwerk
Europop: Church Gift Shop Boys
country: The Sons of Zebedee
surf rock: The Cru-surf-ixions

Kid-focused Christiana

"Cool" Christians often attempt to indoctrinate young children with shoddy, Christ-tinged imitations of the things that kids actually like:

- baseball-card-style "Famous Slaves of the Bible" trading cards and gum
- comic book adventures of religious-themed superheroes like Bible-Man (who wears tights and quotes Jesus), Holy Diver (who maintains a secret identity as Ronny James Dio), and Captain Crucifixion (who cannot be injured except at the sites of the bloody stigmata on his hands and feet)
- animated tales involving sentient, Christ-believing vegetables
- claymation shows about talking Lutheran dogs
- Japanimation Bibles that convey the ability to time travel (but only to Biblical events)
- secret kids-only clubhouses where Bible lessons are taught by walking foam "supercomputers" with piano-keyboard stomachs

These hilariously inept attempts at producing popular culture typically fail to appeal to kids, because either they are only sold at church, they have abysmally poor production values, they can only be seen on low-powered UHF stations at odd hours, or all three. As a result, they have never achieved the mindshare of a "Teenage Mutant Ninja Turtles" or a "Yu-Gi-Oh" or a "Dungeons and Dragons." This makes "cool" Christianity not only false, but also a little bit sad.

39

Some obligatory words about Thomas Kinkade and Joel Osteen

Thomas Kinkade is a factory in California that mass-produces glowy faux-impressionist paintings with Christian and patriotic themes. Joel Osteen is an effeminate megachurch preacher who dispenses feel-good self-help platitudes in a cavernous former basketball arena (and on television) every Sunday. What they have in common is that each uses the implication of religion to sell paintings and books and CDs almost wholly devoid of religious content.

Before being beset by accusations of debatably un-Christian practices like breast-groping, drunken shouting at Siegfried and Roy, and "marking his territory" with urine, Kinkade presided over a fearsome empire of lithography, greeting cards, touch-up craftsmen, in-mall Signature Galleries, and inspirational coffee mugs. According to legend, he used to wander through his facilities shouting "Paint the Light! PAINT THE LIGHT!" although this may be an embellishment created for his made-for-TV biopic, *My Little Kinkadee*. Kinkade's paintings are especially popular with Conservative Protestants, who praise them as "accessible," "unchallenging," and "insipid."

Osteen's message consists of variations on the basic theme "God wants you to be rich," which he emphasizes with non-religious reasoning like "You'll never be what you ought to be if you play it safe" and "I feel like you're supposed to prosper" and "Don't sell the steak, sell the sizzle." Starting with nothing but the megachurch bequeathed to him by his father, Osteen has built a non-denominational, nominally-Christian juggernaut of television shows, bestselling books, appearances on Barbara Walters's "Ten Most Fascinating People" list, and programs to help people reach their "full potential."

Christianity and marketing

In short, whether your product actually has anything to do with religion or not, selling it as pro-Christian can be a valuable marketing tactic. (My publisher pushed really, really hard for this book to be titled "Prosper with the Light Sizzle of Jesus," and relented only after a series of ugly late-night shouting matches.) You are probably familiar with a number of Christian-only-in-a-marketing-sense successes:

- "lose weight fast" diets based on papal edicts
- Chuck Norris
- Creed's first album
- Barack Obama (according to my atheist friend who voted for him)
- MC Hammer's "Pray"
- Chick-Fil-A
- WWJD Bracelets
- the Wake Forest Demon Deacons
- Santa Claus
- movies where Whoopi Goldberg dresses up as a nun

If you aspire to become wealthy, and you don't want to go to all the trouble of starting your own religion from scratch (which, I'm told, requires an obscene variety of permits and applications and licenses), selling to Christians is not a bad path to follow.

RELIGIONS FOUNDED BY MOHAMMED

40

Mohammed and the mountain

Mohammed, also known as Muhammad, Muhammed, Mohammo, Mo-mo, Muumuu, Hambone, Ahmad, The Prophet, The Cheerful One, The Iron Sheikh, Cassius Clay, and pbuh (poo-boo), was born in the sixth century in the city of Mecca in Arabia, a region of the Middle East whose exports include hummus, oil, sand, and terrorists, and whose imports include indentured servants and just about everything else.

At the time Mecca was full of polytheists and idolators whose principal (but absentee) god was Allah, but who also worshipped hundreds of other gods, including (possibly) Chickpea and Garbanzo, the twin gods of hummus; Petrol and Bitumen, the twin gods of oil; Silica, god of sand; Mujahid and Fedayee, the twin gods of terrorism; and Mukataba, the god of human trafficking.

Mohammed's father died a year or two before he was born. Although his mother was still alive, in accordance with tradition Mohammed entered the Arabian foster care system, where (after a delightful series of stereotypical "ragtag family of multi-ethnic foster kids work through their trust issues and learn to cooperate and love and play pranks" adventures that were the basis for a very popular ABC after-school special) he grew up strong and became a prosperous trader and when he was 25 married the wealthy 40-year-old widow Khadijah (from the Arabic for "cougar").

Seizures and hallucinations

Like most men married to substantially older women, Mohammed began spending several weeks each year in a cave, watching cricket matches and meditating. After one too many of his "nag-free vacations," Mohammed began having seizures and imagining that the angel Gabriel was communicating with him.

"Mohammed," one of these hallucinations might have begun, "the end of the world will occur in 28 days, 6 hours, 42 minutes, and 12 seconds." "Also," another probably started, "Chickpea and Garbanzo are false gods, as most likely is Bitumen." "There is no god but Allah," a third may have claimed, "And you, Mo-Mo, are his messenger."

Eventually Mohammed began to discuss these delusions with his family and friends, who (probably as part of the "scrapbooking" craze then in vogue) compiled them into the holy book known as the Qur'an (also called "Al-Qur'an," "Koran," "Alkoran," "Alderaan," and "Also-ran").

Khadijah, her judgment likely impaired by her geriatric state, was the first to accept Mohammed as a prophet, and she was quickly joined by his not-very-critical 10-year-old cousin Ali, his best friend Abu Bakr, and his adopted son Zaid. From this meager core of supporters, Mohammed expanded his following by offering to stick up for the beta males of Mecca, who were tired of having sand kicked in their faces by the ruling idol-worshippers and polytheists. A controversy involving Salman Rushdie's novel *The Satanic Verses* further soured relations between Mohammed and the Meccans.

Funky Cold Medina

Soon afterward, Khadijah died (probably of old age), as did Mohammed's uncle Abu, who had been protecting Mohammed from the legions of disgruntled Bitumen-worshippers. After the *Isra* (an acid-trip during which he hallucinated a visit to Jerusalem) and the *Mi'raj* (an acid trip during which he hallucinated a visit to Disneyland), Mohammed decided it was time to leave Mecca. In the interest of self-preservation, he and the rest of the Muslims fled to the pricey suburb of Medina, where Mohammed wrote a Constitution ensuring speedy trials, blood money, and brutal punishment for poets who mock Islam.

Lonely without Khadijah, Mohammed accumulated a dozen or so replacement wives. (An exact count is hard to come by, since several of them may have only been concubines.) His favorite wife was supposedly Aisha, possibly because they married when she was only seven, meaning he got to play with all of her dollies. As Mohammed was a holy man, he waited until she turned nine before consummating the marriage.

Muhammad quickly launched a series of wars against his neighbors, interpreting every victory as evidence of Allah's divine support and every loss as evidence of Allah's divine support. After years of fighting, the Muslims eventually gathered enough forces to conquer Mecca with minimal bloodshed, killing only a handful of people who were reputed to have drawn cartoons depicting Mohammed.

Mohammed died soon afterward, but not before delivering a farewell sermon in which he encouraged Muslims to emulate the religious faith "of older women," insisted that Muslims live their lives according to the Qur'an "no matter how obsolete new developments in science or technology might render it," and instituted a death tax (over the vehement objections of Steve Forbes).

41

Sunni and Shi'a

Despite being a prophet, Mohammed forgot to appoint a successor, which fractured his followers into two main groups after his death. Over 80% of the world's Muslims are Sunni, so-called because they follow the *Sunnah*, or example set by Mohammed. Sunnis believe that Mohammed's BFF Abu Bakr (Arabic for "Ginger Baker") was elected to be the first Caliph, a non-stick pan made of durable anodized aluminum. He was succeeded by the Caliphs Umar, Uthman, and Ali. Sunnis believe that only these first four Caliphs were "rightly guided," and that subsequent Caliphs lost their way by allowing Muslims to invent coffee, cobwork, and cosmetic dentistry.

Most of the remaining Muslims are Shia, meaning "follower [of Ali]." Shiites believe that the Imams, comprising Mohammed's descendants and David Bowie's wife, have "special spiritual significance," and that Ali, being both Mohammed's cousin and Mohammed's son-in-law, was doubly significant. Accordingly, Shiites believed that Ali should have been the first Caliph, and got very pissy when he wasn't. After Ali's murder, the Shiites insisted that only his descendants were qualified to be Caliph, based on Mohammed's Hadith of the Pond Khumm:

> If I am someone's mawla then Ali is his mawla too.

Although no one has any idea what this means, Shiites tend to offer it as proof that Mohammed wanted only Ali and Ali's progeny to succeed him, while Sunnis consider it merely a missing verse from a Skee-Lo song.

The death of Ali

After Ali was poisoned (and was secretly buried in the Tomb of Imam Ali in the Imam Ali Mosque so that his not-very-bright enemies would be unable to find and desecrate his grave), the Muslims descended into a variety of ugly civil wars that spawned a number of timeless sayings including "I have not yet begun to fight," "One if by sand, two if by sea,"

"Damn the camels, full speed ahead!" and "A Caliphate, if you can keep it."

Sunnis began following the Caliphs while Shiites followed the Imams. The first eleven Imams were all assassinated, poisoned, or beheaded, and sometimes all three. Discerning a pattern, the twelfth Imam, Muhammad al-Mahdi, mysteriously vanished at the precocious age of five. With the benefit of hindsight it is easy to see that he probably wandered off and was eaten by some sort of Sarlacc; however, credulous Shiites imagine that he's still alive centuries later and will probably return at some point. (I wouldn't hold my breath.)

The last Caliph was Mehmet V, who died at the end of World War I. As part of the war's aftermath, the Ottoman Empire dissolved and was replaced by the Republic of Turkey, and the Caliphate was abolished in 1924.

Reestablishing the Caliphate

In recent years, a number of Muslims have called for the reunification of Muslim lands and the reestablishment of the Caliphate, perhaps in a more modern form like Christian-Democratic Caliphate or Compassionate-Conservative Caliphate or Socialism-in-One Caliphate. Muslim organizations devoted to a new Caliphate include Muslim Brotherhood, Muslim Sisterhood, al-Qaeda ("All Your Base"), Tanzeem-e-Islami ("Islamic Dancers"), and Hizb ut-Tahrir ("Party People"). These groups have adopted a variety of re-Caliphatization tactics including terrorism, editorial cartoons, political intimidation, infomercials, anti-Americanism, suicide bombings, study circles, plane-hijackings, and visiting Colorado as an exchange student.

Modern-day Sunni-Shia relations

Ever since the 1980 release of the Cure's *Boys Don't Cry* album, Shiites and Sunnis have found themselves in frequent conflict, even in normally peaceful countries like Iraq, Jordan, Pakistan, Syria, Yemen, and Afghanistan.

Depending on what sort of conspiracy theorist you are, these conflicts were driven by "Jewish interests," the song "Killing an Arab," the Islamic revolution in Iran, the "new world order," close American ties to Saudi Arabia, or blood-drinking reptilian humanoids from Alpha Draconis. Nonetheless, given all the things they hate in common, the prospects for rapprochement are looking good!

42

Islam is false

Mohammed's religion is nowadays called Islam, meaning "submission." Not, mind you, the exciting kind of submission, like when you send your short story about the kid who wants to play baseball but is no good at it to the literary magazine published by some obscure small college in Nebraska, or when you email the proposal for your anti-religion polemic to every literary agent you can find on the internet and then never hear back from any of them. No, Islam means "submission to Allah," who has no interest in your short stories (let alone your heresies) and mostly wants you to live in the desert and form oil cartels and not have five wives.

Islam currently has over a billion followers, which makes it the world's second largest religion after Christianity.

The five pillars

Although there are many varieties of Islam, there are five widely-agreed-upon "pillars" of the religion:

1. Shahadah

The most important ("load-bearing") pillar, shahadah refers to the required daily profession of faith: "There is no god but god, and there is no Mohammed but Mohammed, and there is no business like show business, and there is no spoon. There is no spoon? Then you will see, it is not the spoon that bends, it is only yourself."

2. Salah

Muslims are required to pray five times a day: during "Good Morning America," at lunch, before "Oprah," after "Oprah," and when flipping back and forth between "Leno" and "Letterman." These prayers should be prayed while kneeling on bathmats and facing toward Mecca, after washing one's feet in a public restroom sink.

3. Zakaat

Muslims are required to donate to charity. Zakaat is typically calculated as a fixed percentage of income, with a complicated schedule of deductions for things like third wives, camel payments, using part of one's tent as a home office, and medical expenses exceeding a certain threshold.

4. Sawm

During the month of Ramadan, Muslims are required to fast from sunrise to sunset. Unlike the "cleansing fast" your colon hydrotherapist prescribed, the Sawm requires abstaining from food, drink, sexual activity, showering, video games, haircuts, signaling left turns, changing light bulbs, and pay-per-view movies.

5. Hajj

At least once in his life, every Muslim is supposed to travel to Mecca during the month of Dhu al-Hijjah, when airfares are typically lowest. Although this pilgrimage is an ancient tradition, the Hajj has in recent years become big business and now includes a variety of for-pay extras such as head-shaving, devil-stoning, funnel cakes, walking in circles, and pilgrim-trampling.

The houses

Traditional Islam views the world as divided into two "houses" – the Dar al-Islam ("house of peace," the countries ruled by Islamic law) and the Dar al-Harb ("house of war," the countries not yet forced under the rule of Islamic law). Some more nuanced Muslims add additional houses, including Dar al-Hudna ("the house of infidels who pay us tribute for not killing them"), Dar al-'Ahd ("the house of infidels who we're afraid of and so we have a treaty with"), Dar al-Ftirah ("the house of pies"), Dar al-Dawa ("the house of infidels who have never heard of Islam"), and Dar al-Amn ("the house of infidels who cheerfully invite a fifth column of Muslims to live there and plant the seeds for eventual Islamic rule"). Although it is not universally accorded pillar status, Islam also puts great importance on the notion of jihad, or struggle between these houses.

Sharia law

Besides these pillars, there is a huge amount of *sharia* law covering every-thing from how to kill unbelievers, to how to kill apostates, to how to kill disrespectful family members. Sharia is based on a combination of the Qur'an (the holy texts revealed to Mohammed), the hadith (teachings that sound like something Mohammed might have said), Ijma ("if-by-whiskey" arguments), Qiyas ("straw men"), and Aql ("loaded questions"). Although sharia is pretty all-encompassing, the following should give you an idea of life as an observant Muslim.

banking: Muslims are forbidden to pay *riba*, or interest on loans. As a result, no one ever wants to lend them money, and they end up having to buy everything from shady rent-to-own places that advertise on TV.

marriage: Muslim men are allowed to have no more than four wives. However, wives taken as *nikah mut'ah* (from the Arabic for "fixed-duration temporary sex spouse") don't count towards the limit. Muslim women are generally allowed only one husband each; how-ever, a married female slave may also marry her owner (which is pretty much just common sense).

loss prevention: If you steal from a Muslim, he is supposed to cut off your hands. If you have no hands (perhaps from previous thefts, or from a lawnmower accident), he is supposed to cut off your nose, and so on. No matter how many things you steal, you still get to keep your ears, and I'll tell you why. So that every shriek of every child at seeing your hideousness will be yours to cherish. Every babe that weeps at your approach, every woman who cries out, "Dear God! What is that thing," will echo in your perfect ears. It means he leaves you in anguish, wallowing in freakish misery forever. (He will not, however, file an insurance claim for the theft, as insurance is prohibited under sharia.)

toilet etiquette: Unlike one of my co-workers whom I will not name, Muslims are forbidden to talk on cell phones while going to the bathroom. After finishing their business, they are required to pray: "Praise be to Allah who relieved me of the filth, made my bladder gladder, found me a man to see about a horse, led the Browns to the Super Bowl, downloaded my brownload, pumped a clump of dump out of my rump, pinch-hit for Kurt Bevacqua, took the Cosby kids to the pool, and gave me relief."

dhimmi tax: Non-Muslims living under Muslim rule are required to pay *jizya*, a fee to help defray the costs of allowing them to practice their own religions.

alcohol: Muslims are forbidden not only from drinking and brewing alcohol, but also from selling it, transporting it in their taxi cabs, using it in their onion-ring batter, creating dice games involving it, and blending it with gasoline to fill up their flexible-fuel vehicles.

wudu: Before they pray, Muslims are supposed to perform a partial ablution called *wudu*, based on the Cole Porter lyric "Do do that wudu that you do so well."

dogs: According to Sunni tradition, Mohammed was afraid of dogs. As a result Islam considers dogs to be ritually unclean animals with the power to "void wudu" (though some dissident Muslims argue that wudu can only really void itself).

pork: Muslims are not allowed to "dig on swine." Some of Mohammed's contemporaries pointed out to him that "bacon tastes goooood," to which he famously responded: "Hey, sewer rat may taste like pumpkin pie, but I'd never know 'cause I wouldn't eat the filthy motherfucker. Pigs sleep and root in shit. That's a filthy animal. I ain't eat nothin' that ain't got enough sense enough to disregard its own feces."

cartoons: If there's one thing that Mohammed hated more than having his picture taken, it was having his caricature drawn. To respect his wishes, devout Muslims not only refrain from producing Mohammed drawings and cartoons and paintings but also deliver death threats to Mohammed-depicting artists, set fire to the local embassies of the home countries of Mohammed-depicting artists, desecrate the national flags of Mohammed-depicting artists, and boycott the gallery openings of Mohammed-depicting artists.

Muslims also have specialized dress codes. Men are encouraged to wear business-casual attire and nappy-looking beards, while women are expected to "guard their modesty." Depending on the specific implementation of Islamic law, women can be required to wear veils, headscarves, trucker hats, baggy sweatpants, ninja costumes, or ski masks. Even in non-Islamic countries, many Muslim women choose (usually under pressure from their families and threats of being doused with acid) to wear these outfits. Occasionally they even write op-ed pieces explaining how the veil "liberates" them from being treated as sex objects, which helps explain the near-equal status attained by women in most Islamic countries (and, in particular, the fact that women are nowadays allowed to drive in a majority of such countries).

Terrorism

A small minority of Muslims seem to have gotten the impression somewhere that Islamic theology encourages violence. And it's true that a tiny handful of organizations like Al-Qaeda, Abu Hafs al-Masri Brigades, The Abu Sayyaf Group, The Aden-Abyan Islamic Army, Al-Badr, al-Gama'a al-Islamiyya, Al-Shabaab, Ansar al-Islam, The Armed Islamic Group, East Turkestan Islamic Movement, East Turkestan Liberation Organization, Eritrean Islamic Jihad, Fatah al-Islam, The Great Eastern Islamic Raiders' Front, Harkat-ul-Jihad-al-Islami, Harkat-ul-Mujahideen-al-Islami, Hezb-e-Islami Gulbuddin, Hezbollah Al-Hejaz, Hisbi Islam, Hizb-an-Nusra, Hizb-e-Abu Omar, Hizbul Mujahideen, Indian Mujahideen, Ingush Jamaat, Islamic Army in Iraq, Islamic Front for Armed Jihad, Islamic Jihad Movement in Palestine, Islamic Jihad Organization, Islamic Jihad Union, Islamic Jihad for the Liberation of Palestine, Islamic Movement of Central Asia, Islamic Movement of Kurdistan, Islamic Movement of Uzbekistan, Islamic State of Iraq, Jagrata Muslim Janata Bangladesh, Jaish-e-Mohammed, Jama'at al-Jihad al-Islami, Jama'at al-Tawhid wal-Jihad, Jamaat Ansar al-Sunna, Jamaat ul-Fuqra, Jemaah Islamiyah, Kataib al-Khoul, Lashkar-e-Islam, Lashkar-e-Jhangvi, Lashkar-e-Omar, Lashkar-e-Taiba, Laskar Jihad, Libyan Islamic Fighting Group, Maktab al-Khidamat, Markaz Dawa-Wal-Irshad, Moro Islamic Liberation Front, Moroccan Islamic Combatant Group, Mujahedeen KOMPAK, Mujahideen Army, Mujahideen Shura Council, Muslim Brotherhood, Safdar Nagori, Shariat Jamaat, Sipah-e-Sahaba Pakistan, Students Islamic Movement of India, Takfir wal-Hijra, Taliban, Turkish Hezbollah, Union of Mujahidin, United Jihad Council, and Yarmuk Jamaat have in recent years engaged in nominally-Islamic, violent acts.

I'm sure you've probably heard sensationalized accounts of their crimes, possibly including the July 2006 Srinagar bombings, the August 2005 Bangladesh bombings, the 1980 Paris synagogue bombing, the 1981 Antwerp bombing, the 1981 Vienna synagogue attack, the 1983 Kuwait bombings, the 1993 CIA shootings, the 1993 World Trade Center bombing, the 1995 Rijeka bombing, the 1997 Sangrampora massacre, the 1998 Chamba massacre, the 1998 Coimbatore bombings, the 1998 Prankote massacre, the 1998 Wandhama massacre, the 2000 Amarnath pilgrimage massacre, the 2001 Chalwalkote massacre, the 2001 Indian Parliament attack, the 2001 Jammu and Kashmir legislative assembly attack, the 2001 Kishtwar massacre, the 2002 Bali bombings, the 2002 Kaluchak massacre, the 2002 Qasim Nagar massacre, the 2002 Qasimnagar massacre of Kashmiri Pandits, the 2003 Casablanca bombings, the 2003 Nadimarg Massacre, the 2004 Australian embassy bombing in Jakarta, the 2004 Khobar massacre, the 2004 Madrid train bombings, the 2004 Teli Katha massacre, the 2005 Alexandria riot, the 2006 Central Mindanao bombings, the 2006 Doda massacre, the 2006 Kulgam massacre, the 2006 Varanasi bombings, the 2008 Agartala bombings, the 2008 Ahmedabad bombings, the 2005 London bombings, the 2008 Delhi blast, the Akshardham Temple attack, the 2007 Baghlan sugar factory bombing, the 2005 Bali bombings, the Bangalore bombings, the 2007 Basilan beheading incident, the Bojinka plot, the 2007 Casablanca bombings, the Chittisinghpura massacre, the Christmas Eve 2000 Indonesia bombings, the Cinema Rex fire, the 2006 Dahab bombings, the Haifa bus 37 suicide bombing, the Jaffa Road bus bombings, the 2008 Kandahar bombing, the 2002 Karachi bus bombing, the Karachi consulate attacks, the Khobar Towers bombing, the Lebanon hostage crisis, the Luxor massacre, the 2006 Malegaon blasts, the 2003 Marriott Hotel bombing, the Mercaz HaRav massacre, the July 2006 Mumbai train bombings, the Riyadh compound bombings, the September 11 attacks, the 2004 Sinai bombings, the Spin Boldak bombing, and the 2002 Zamboanga bombing, just to name a few.

According to other Muslims, however, the sky-man Allah frowns on televised beheadings of kidnappees. What's more, the Qur'an is a "book of peace" that the few Muslim terrorists have all coincidentally misinterpreted in the exact same way. And, while violence is "never justified," we should be more sympathetic to their legitimate grievances, like the fact that our women are encouraged to wear bikinis on TV while theirs are expected to hide under heavy, shape-concealing blankets.

Nonetheless, there is no excuse for terrorism; the veil liberates no one; pork is exceptionally tasty; rent-to-own is a huge rip-off; praying five times a day is a huge waste of time; and there is no god Allah. Islam is false.

43

Salafism is false

Salafism is a popular movement within Sunni Islam based on the desire to live like *salaf* ("cave people"). Salafis believe that Islam was at its most complete and perfect sometime in the early 7th century, and that people should live by the examples set by the first few generations of Muslims:

- Believed in demons
- Lived without electricity
- Considered musical instruments "wicked"
- Wouldn't celebrate Mohammed's birthday
- Banned critical discussion of religious dogma
- Refused to watch any TV that was not Al-Jazeera

Mohammed's own words are usually invoked as justification:

> Whoever innovates or accommodates an innovator then upon him is the curse of Allah, His Angels and the whole of mankind.

This quote is also offered as an explanation of why so few Muslims receive patents, why the Arabic translation of *Atlas Shrugged* sells so poorly, why the Muslim world adamantly refuses to recognize the achievements of Thomas Edison, and why so many Muslim countries are backward hellholes.

Youth appeal

Salafism has in recent times grown popular with disaffected Muslim youth around the world, for reasons like "it makes me feel like a man," "it's a way of sticking it to my parents," and "setting the trappings of modern civilization on fire is fun!" Saudi Arabia, whose dominant Wahhabi Islam is a flavor of Salafism, has used its vast oil wealth to fund the worldwide spread of Wahhabism, mostly by distributing pamphlets arguing that "infidels suck," opening Islamic madrasas that teach controversial topics like phonics and hatred of non-Muslims, and offering flight-school scholarships to aspiring hijackers.

Ironically, the Salafis tend to use all of the modern inventions they purport to hate, like Rolls-Royces, Molotov cocktails, YouTube, and iPods. If even its supposed believers don't follow it, then clearly Salafism is false.

44

Sufism is false

Like other religions, Islam has its mystics, called Sufis. Sufism (also called "Tasawwuf") is based on the idea that ordinary mental tools like logic and observation and common sense are insufficient to understand god, and that the devout should instead rely on New Age concepts like "spiritual striving," "knowledge of the heart," and "inner journeys."

The word Sufi is derived from the Arabic words *safa* ("pure") and *suf* ("wool"), and most likely refers to the prophet Mohammed's favorite sweater, a green cardigan from Banana Republic. Sufis are required to join spiritual orders, called *tariqa*, and to have spiritual mentors, whom they usually meet at local Boys and Girls Clubs. The Sufis are perhaps best known for their spiritual practice of "whirling," spinning in circles until they are so nauseated that they can transcend their evil desires, replacing them with the holy desire to blow chunks, to pray at the porcelain altar, to drive the big white bus, or to yawn in Technicolor.

Sufi Poetry

Sufis are also famous for their poetry. Some of the best-loved Sufi poems are *Turyaaq-e-Qulb* ("O Caliph! My Caliph!"), *Diwan-e Shams-e Tabrizi* ("Stopping by Dunes on a Sandy Evening"), *Kimiya-yi Sa'adat* ("There Once Was a Sheikh from Nantucket"), and *Dala'il al-Barakat* ("The Love Song of J. Abu Bakr"). In order to really understand Sufism, I experimented with writing my own religious poetry:

> There once was a man from Medina,
> Who was an interior designer.
>   Despite sex in the butt,
>   He's not "People of Lut."
> He's just terrified of the vagina!

So he went on a great Hajj to Mecca
Where he met a young girl named Rebecca.
When she showed him her yoni,
He sprang pepperoni
And discovered a new home for his pecker.

Then they went to al-Quds al-Sharif
Where he injected her with his beef.
He tithed his zakaat
In her warm honeypot
And stole off in the night like a thief.

Incredibly, this poem was rejected by all the leading literary journals, including *Sufi Review*, *The Prophet*, *Tasawwuf Poetics*, and *Bayazid Bastami's Internet Tendency*.

Other prominent Sufi practices include stabbing yourself with knives, stabbing yourself with awls, stabbing yourself with daggers, stabbing yourself with swords, stabbing yourself with high-heeled shoes, and attributing the glory to god if you manage to survive.

Most Sunnis and Shiites don't think much of Sufis, arguing that they violate Quranic proscriptions against "stabbing yourself," "vomiting," and "writing bad poetry." Furthermore, the growing popularity of MTV's "Jackass" has diminished the shock value of Sufi stunts. Youth interest in Sufism has fallen off accordingly, and the future of Sufism is unclear. Not that it matters, since there is no such thing as "knowledge of the heart" or "inner journeys," and Sufism is false.

RELIGIONS THAT MAY OR MAY NOT BE CHRISTIANITY, DEPENDING ON WHOM YOU ASK

45

Messianic Judaism is false

Thematically this chapter could have been included with "Religions of the Jews," but it should be much more understandable here, with the story of Jesus already under our belts. (Also, my Jewish friends would never forgive me if I put it in the "Jews" chapter.)

Messianic Jews (some of whom call themselves "Jews for Jesus," others of whom wouldn't call themselves "Jews for Jesus" if you paid them) believe that Jesus was the messiah that other Jews are still waiting for. Like Christians, they believe in the divinity of Jesus; like Jews, they avoid eating cheeseburgers. This is based on the belief that Paul, founder of the church, never abandoned Judaism:

> Then Paul, knowing that some of them were Sadducees and the others Pharisees, called out in the Sanhedrin, "My brothers, I am a Pharisee, the son of a Pharisee.
>
> Acts 23:6

(The passage is easier to understand if you know that the Pharisees were the ancestors of today's Jews, and that the Sanhedrin was the ancient Israeli equivalent of today's "People's Court.")

Messianism

Messianics object to the division of the Bible into Old Testament and New Testament, preferring the terms "Bible Classic" and "New Bible." In order not to scare off potential Jewish converts, Messianics have their own set of euphemisms for common Christian terms:

Christian-speak	Messianic-speak
Jesus	"Yeshua"
god the father	"Colonel Goddo"
god the holy spirit	"Doctor Goddenstein"
baptism	"mikveh"
apostles	"minyan"
cross	"big wooden T"
crucifixion	"just hanging"
John the Baptist	"Yochanan the Mensch"
church	"Jew house"

Messianic Jews spread their faith using colorful brochures, tacky t-shirts, and aggressive pamphleteers. They also have a TV station, "God's Learning Channel," that can be seen in certain remote parts of Texas if you have a really powerful antenna.

But as Jesus was not divine, and as cheeseburgers are incredibly tasty, Messianic Judaism is doubly false.

46

Religions that claim to be science are false

As we have repeatedly seen, pretty much all religions make claims that conflict with science (e.g. "sea spontaneously parts," "crucified criminal rises from dead to wreak hellish revenge," "survivor of planetary explosion develops super-strength when exposed to light of yellow sun"). Many religions insist that therefore science must be wrong. Other religions claim that this conflict is in fact illusory. And a third set of religions actually claim to be science themselves.

The most well-known example is probably Christian Science, although there are also small numbers of believers in Jewish Science, Zoroastrian Science, Giant Stone Head Worship Science, and Christian Scientist Science.

Mary Baker Eddy

Christian Science was formed by Mary Baker Eddy, who, despite her name, was neither a baker nor an eddy. In 1866 she slipped and fell and was severely injured, leading to the Christian Science creed "I've fallen, and I can't get up!" After reading about Jesus faith-healing a paralytic and also after her friends kept telling her to "stop faking," she miraculously recovered (although she also miraculously waited a long time before withdrawing her slippery floor lawsuit against Walmart).

She next spent three years studying the Bible, during which she concluded that since Jesus healed people without (having access to and therefore without) using medicine or science, so should we. (She remained oddly silent on the similar fact that Jesus crapped without having access to indoor plumbing.) Eddy published these revelations in her opus *Science and Health: Both For Chumps*, later republished as *Science and Health: Jesus Didn't Know About Them, So Neither Should You.*

Eventually she founded the Christian Science Church and its associated periodicals, including the *Christian Science Sentinel*, the *Christian Science Monitor*, *Cosmo-Christian-Science-Politan*, *The New Christian Science Yorker*, and *Christian Science Highlights for Kids*.

The practice of Christian Science

Christian Scientists believe that god has made all things "in his likeness," which would mean that he was somehow both as attractive as Ashley Olsen and as terrifying-looking as Mary-Kate Olsen. They also follow Mary Baker Eddy's teachings to eschew medicine in favor of "Christian Science treatment," which mostly involves prayer, refusing blood transfusions, and dying.

Christian Scientists may be best known for the reading rooms they maintain all over the world that provide Christian Science literature to interested persons and to homeless people looking for a dry place to sit. Some of the nicer reading rooms now have espresso stands, free wifi, and DVD rentals.

However, you can get all these same perks at the public library, plus they'll check you out books on taboo topics like surgery and pharmaceuticals and *real* science. And as Mary Baker Eddy was not a prophet of god but merely a crazy old woman with crazy old woman stories and a crazy old woman smell, Christian Science is false, and so are all the other religious sciences.

47

Religions that leave tracts in the laundromat on 12th Avenue are false

When I mention "watchtower," what comes to mind? If you're like most people, you think of the Bob Dylan / Jimi Hendrix Experience / U2 / Prince / Neil Young / Pearl Jam / Battlestar Galactica hit "All Along the Watchtower." If you're the type of dork who lines up bright and early every Wednesday morning to get first crack at the week's new comic books, you probably think of the Justice League's orbiting headquarters. And if you're a forest ranger (or Smokey Bear), you're probably remembering all the summers you wasted sitting in a little wooden room 100 feet above the ground, scouring the woods all day for early signs of wildfires, while your friends were living in that beach house in San Diego, smoking weed, meeting girls, catching rays, and learning to surf.

But maybe you used to live on 12th Avenue, and you used to wash your clothes at Coin-op Carnival, and each weekend while you waited for dryers to become available you used to leaf through the stacks of fourth-rate reading material that people had left lying around, and every Sunday you ended up with the latest copy of *Watchtower*, the official propaganda magazine of Jehovah's Witnesses.

"Don't Taze me bro!"

In the late 1800's, Charles "Taze" Russell placed a personal ad in an alterna-weekly offering himself as a "faithful and discreet slave." After smoothing things over with the legions of disappointed responders, he founded the Watch Tower Society, whose teachings departed from traditional Christian doctrine in several ways:

- Jesus invisibly returned to earth in 1874, started the great Tom Collins hoax, and helped debunk John Ernst Worrell Keely's etheric generator as a thermodynamically-impossible perpetual motion machine.

- World War I represented the beginning of Armageddon, Satan's plan to destroy the earth with a giant asteroid.
- The Great Pyramid of Giza was *not* one of the Seven Wonders of the Ancient World; rather, Snofru's Red Pyramid was.
- Jesus did not die on a cross; this is a mistranslation. He died on a large, wooden T.

After his mysterious death on a train, his followers removed the space from "Watchtower" and rebranded themselves as Jehovah's Witnesses. JeWits meet for worship in buildings called Kingdom Halls, a name most likely taken from a Stephen King miniseries.

They are well-known for their extremely active door-to-door prose-lytization. Their most prolific converters are eligible to win prizes like inflatable rafts, baseball gloves, *Dick Tracy* cameras, chemistry sets, air rifles, electric phonographs, field glasses, sleeping bags, ukuleles, and crystal radio kits. As mentioned above, they also produce a wide variety of proselytizing magazines, which they leave in laundromats and courthouses and airports and anywhere else that people have to wait around doing nothing for long periods of time.

Socially, they oppose most of the same things as Conservative Protestants, like abortion and immodesty and dancing and fun. JeWits believe that the earth is secretly ruled by the invisible Satan, who misleads people into purchasing things they don't need like Showtime Rotisseries, Mr. Microphones, and Veg-o-Matics.

Jehovah's Witnesses are not allowed to serve in the military, to sing the national anthem, or to use American Flag stamps on letters, out of a belief that nationalism might interfere with their proselytization. They also avoid celebrating birthdays, Mother's Day, and Thanksgiving, which they consider festivals celebrating pagan gods. Based on Biblical passages loosely implying that the primary purpose of blood is "atonement for one's sins," JeWits famously eschew blood donations, blood transfusions, blood pudding, blood sausage, *czernina*, *dinuguan*, Black Soup, menstruation, rare steaks, vampirism, and hemophilia.

Jesus, though, did not return to earth in 1874 (and certainly played no role in the Collins hoax), rare steaks are the tastiest, and an actual discreet slave wouldn't try to force his religion on you. Jehovah's Witnesses is false.

48

Twelve-step programs are false

Alcohol is tasty and charm-enhancing. It helps build confidence and takes the edge off some of the too-painful-to-deal-with aspects of life. It eases social interactions and helps people fit in with their peers. It often makes problems simply vanish!

Despite these benefits, it turns out there are some people who wish to consume less alcohol! Many of them have joined Alcoholics Anonymous, a religious fellowship that promises to end your drinking in twelve easy steps, many of which involve Colonel Goddo:

2. Decide that only belief in the invisible sky-man can restore your sanity.
3. Devote your life to the sky-man.
5. Tell the sky-man about your failings.
6. Get ready to let the sky-man improve you.
7. Humbly ask the sky-man to improve you.
11. Use prayer and meditation to improve contacts with the sky-man.
12. Sign up your friends.

Scientific studies quickly demonstrated that Alcoholics Anonymous was not particularly effective at curbing the desire to drink sweet, sweet bourbon. Nonetheless, it was found terrifically effective at recruiting new members to sign up for Alcoholics Anonymous. Part of this growth has involved applying the twelve steps to other habits, resulting in groups like Clutterers Anonymous, Crystal Meth Anonymous, Emotions Anonymous, Mopery Anonymous, Sexaholics Anonymous, Scientologists Anonymous, Online Gamers Anonymous, Chocoholics Anonymous, Cough-Syrup-holics Anonymous, Glue-Huffers Anonymous, and Identity-Concealers Anonymous.

New Twelve-steppers are typically paired with a sponsor who can help them get past their resistance to the steps involving belief in the implausible Goddo, and who can provide sexual favors to help distract from the often overwhelming desire to "take just one more sip." Twelve-steppers commonly encourage each other to "let go and let god," which doesn't make any sense but sounds clever if you don't think about it too hard.

There is, of course, no sky-man, and if there were there's no way he'd want to keep you from the life-changing pleasures of whiskey, vicodin, hobbyist cement, or co-dependency. Twelve-step programs are false.

49

Seventh-Day Adventism is false

Years ago a Christian sect known as the Millerites, named for their love of genuine draft beer, taught that Jesus was going to return to earth in the year 1844. Obviously, this did not happen, resulting in an event known as either The Great Disappointment, Shattered Dreams, or "Duh!" Although most of the Millerites abandoned their faith in the face of relentless mocking from their friends and neighbors, a few of them decided that Jesus had actually moved apartments in heaven, which in some hyper-technical sense meant that their prophecies hadn't been wrong.

Rebranding themselves as Seventh-Day Adventists, they sensed an undersupplied market and started holding church services on Saturdays.

Ellen White

The Adventists have 28 fundamental beliefs, which are mostly minor variations on straightforward Protestant dogma, with the exceptions of Belief #24, which promises the faithful "first dibs" on Jesus's heavenly apartment, Belief #28, which asserts the existence of a "twin earth" filled with functionally-identical but chemically-different "water," and Belief #18, which insists that Adventism co-founder Ellen White was actually a prophet who received messages from god the holy spirit.

Critics of Adventism point out that White was a cataleptic hysteric who was prone to fits of automatism, who plagiarized Rose Kennedy's book *Times to Remember*, and who frowned on miscegenation.

As part of their reinterpretation of Christ's 1844 no-show, Adventists developed the idea of "investigative judgment," the belief that the reason Jesus never showed up is that he's hanging out in a "heavenly sanctuary," drinking Millers and participating in a heavenly show trial. Other Christians are critical of this idea, typically on the grounds that "Ellen White made it up, and that lady was nuts."

Skallops and Stripples

Adventists promote vegetarianism and have been responsible for a wide variety of innovative imitation-meats, including FriPats®, Leanies®, Stripples®, Choplets®, Vegetable Skallops®, and (every kid's favorite) Low Fat Veja-Links®. Adventists also believe in the health benefits of breakfast cereal and (through the Adventist-founded Kellogg's) brought the world such beloved treats as Apple Jacks, Froot Loops, Honey Smacks, and C-3PO's.

Nonetheless, Miller is a pretty lousy beer, cataleptic hysterics make pretty lousy prophets, Saturday is a pretty lousy sabbath, and a Jesus who doesn't bother to show up when he says he's going to is a pretty lousy Jesus. Seventh-Day Adventism is false.

50

Quakerism is false

Contrary to popular belief (and hundreds of millions of dollars of marketing), Quaker Oats have nothing to do with Quakers. In fact, they (the oats, not the Quakers) are now a division of PepsiCo, which is currently controlled by Hindus.

Quakerism, which is short for the creepy-sounding "Religious Society of Friends," was founded in the 17th century by the Englishman George Fox. After encountering almost-immediate persecution, the Quakers fled England for the New World. They quickly ran afoul of Massachusetts's Quaker-hanging policy, and they soon left to start their own state in Pennsylvania.

Like many other religions, the Quakers have repeatedly split over doctrinal minutiae, grouping into sects like Hicksites, Plymouth Brethren, Gurneyites, Wilburites, Magicites, Beanites, Dolomites, Parasites, and Frostbites.

Quaking

Friends believe that god needs to be personally experienced, either as an "inner light," an "ingrown Christ," "the evil within," a "space seed," or "the pleasure principle." Although this idea has not really caught on outside of their community, other Friends habits have become popular with non-Quakers, including the catchphrase "How *you* doin'?" the "Rachel" haircut, and the idea of hanging out all day in coffee shops.

Testimonies

While most Christians are content with static Jesus-era dogma, Quakers insist on more recently invented "testimonies," things that every Friend should believe "if he knows what's good for him." Although different sects share different testimonies, the so-called "PESTimonies" are probably the most popular:

Peace: Quakers all acknowledge the prophetic gifts of "Last Night I Had the Strangest Dream" folksinger Ed McCurdy.

Equality: Quakers believe that since all people have the same "divine spark," they all deserve equal treatment. Accordingly, they frown on scientific research investigating whether males and females actually do have the same divine spark, insisting that such questions have no place in the academy.

Simplicity: Friends like to use archaic words like "thee," "thou," "thine," "wouldst," "alack," "betwixt," "forsooth," "prithee," "whence," "methinks," "yon," "ye," and "thy," in order to make their speech sound "simple." In fact, it has the opposite effect.

Truth: Usually summed up as "Pick two: true to god, true to self, true to others."

Quaker worship services are (incredibly) even more boring than other Christian services, as they mostly consist of a bunch of Friends sitting around a room and not saying anything, as poignantly described in the children's rhyme "Quaker Meeting":

Quaker meeting has begun.
No more laughing, no more fun.
If you show your teeth or tongue,
We will stuff your mouth with dung.

This sort of silence also characterizes the "in the manner of Friends" decision process, which is slow and passive and (probably due to some sort of bias) almost never part of Business School curricula.

In any event, there are no such things as inner light (unless you swallow a lantern) or ingrown Christ, and no one likes a PEST. Quakerism is false.

Amishness is false

In 1693, a group of Mennonites who felt their church had gone soft on shunning excommunicants broke away and formed the Amish. They moved to Pennsylvania and Ohio, where most Amish still live today.

Unlike (for instance) Objectivists, the Amish are deeply anti-individualistic, preferring to submit to the Will of God, which refers to "whatever our community says we have to do." They typically gather together at someone's house each Sunday, read the Bible in German, sit around in long stretches of silence, listen to boring sermons, and chant German hymns like "In Heaven There Is No Beer" and "The Chicken Dance."

Plain People

Amish dress plainly, do not drive cars, eschew most uses of high-voltage electricity, keep their telephones in the yard, and refuse to educate their children past the eighth grade, arguing that ninth-grade science might "cause the kids to critically reconsider some of our beliefs."

The media often present the Amish as a rigid monoculture with strict, universal rules. In fact the various Amish communities differ on everything from "how wide must a hat brim be?" to "what color should a buggy be painted?" to "are snaps on clothing permissible, or should we stick with buttons?"

Nonetheless, most Amish teens participate in the *rumspringa*, in which they leave the farm, drive buggies under the influence, move to Los Angeles, film a reality show based on their interactions with shallow Californian kids, become disgusted with the excesses of American mainstream culture, argue with the producers, and then return home to a life of farming and building barns with hand tools.

However, electricity is terrifically useful, shunning is a barbaric practice, buggies may be painted any color, and "In Heaven There Is No Beer" should really only be sung during Oktoberfest. Amishness is false.

Mormonism is false

Mormonism is an offshoot of Christianity founded in the 1800s by Joseph Smith, a treasure-hunter who maintained a secret identity as "the Glass Looker." In 1823, Smith claimed he was visited by the angel Moroni (possibly short for "Moronic"), who led him to a set of cryptic-writing-covered "golden plates" that he conveniently refused to show to anyone. Hiding behind a curtain and using a "seer stone," he managed to translate the writing, which he immediately copyrighted as The Book of Mormon.

Smith quickly established a church, moved to Missouri, started a series of wars, spent some time in prison, and ended up in Illinois, where he began to establish church practices like Sunday Meetings, plural marriage, and destroying his critics. Smith further preached that traditional Christians had lost their way several centuries previous, and that Mormonism represented a return to a true form of Christianity that would allow him to have several wives. Soon afterward, Smith was murdered by local theocracy-phobes, and his replacement Brigham Young moved the church to Utah, where the skiing was better, and where there were fewer blacks to protest Young's policy of banning them from the priesthood.

Over the years, the Mormons have turned Utah into an exceptionally clean, exceptionally boring, exceptionally conservative, exceptionally white state, mostly famous for its Mormon temples, its Grand-Staircase-Escalante monument, its dry-lakebed rocket-car speedway, and its Christa McAuliffe Space Education Center.

The word of wisdom

Mormons are required to live their lives according to the Word of Wisdom, which cannot be revealed to non-Mormons (but which is rumored to be "masticate"). Accordingly, Mormons are prohibited from partaking of wine, tobacco, or "hot drinks" (e.g. Coca-Cola). Mormons are also not supposed to eat meat, "except when slathered with a tangy, vinegar-based sauce," nor refined grain (based on the belief that Moroni suffered from cœliac disease).

Like many other religions, Mormonism forbids pre-marital sex, gay sex, sexual fantasies, auto-erotic asphyxiation, lust, "Barely Legal" magazines, otherkin erotica, and rubbing oneself against a washing machine during spin cycle. "No problem," you're thinking, "I'll just take advantage of the rich sexual variety provided by my several wives!" Unfortunately for you, in the late 1800's, after the federal government outlawed polygamy, the church leaders conveniently received a revelation informing them that plural marriage was no longer an encouraged part of the religion. So that's out, too. However, Mormons are still required to wear magical undergarments that, at various times, have been claimed to "calm the urges," to protect the wearer in the event of a plane crash, and to reduce skid marks.

Missions

After high school, young Mormons are paired up, given quotas, dressed in ill-fitting suits, and sent on multi-year missionary trips to recruit new Mormons around the world. As a result, there are surprisingly many Mormon converts in only-reachable-by-missionary places like Amazon jungles, former Soviet Republics, Antarctica, and Seattle. Also as a result, the seniors at Brigham Young University are several years older than seniors at non-Mormon colleges, giving them a distinct advantage in football. Accordingly, a disproportionate number of professional quarterbacks are Mormons, creating endorsement headaches for Budweiser and Pepsi and *Out* magazine.

Napoleon Dynamite

Mormons specialize in creating quirky, not-particularly-entertaining movies, like *The Book of Mormon Movie, Mobsters and Mormons, Tales of the Rat Fink*, and *Napoleon Dynamite*. They are also quite accomplished at disguising Mormon theology as popular science fiction – *Ender's Game* is a thinly-veiled retelling of Brigham Young's journey to Utah; *Dragonlance* recasts the 1838 Mormon War as a battle between the forces of Tanis Half-Elven and the Death Knight Lord Soth; and the *Twilight* books are a fictionalized account of Joseph Smith's plural marriage to a vampire.

Through their outreach branch, The Church of Jesus Christ of Latter Day Saints, Mormons maintain a campy ad campaign encouraging children to tell the truth when they accidentally break a window, encouraging deadbeat dads to write child-support checks more often, and encouraging gang members not to shoot each other merely on account of "hanging" with the wrong "crew," always summing up their lessons with the Mormon catchphrase "that's one to grow on."

The Mormons are also well-known for their "baptism of the dead" ceremony, in which they use the internet to research your genealogy, dig up your corpse (or mummy, or ashes, or LifeGem®), and posthumously turn you into a Mormon (rendering useless the bottle of whiskey you insisted you be buried with).

Although the mainstream Mormon church has tried to tone down its most outrageous teachings, there are a number of spinoff Latter-Day-Saints churches located in small towns on the Utah border (which, they tell themselves, renders them exempt from the laws of man), with dictatorial prophets who practice polygamy, routinely excommunicate and expel young men who might someday resent their wife-hoarding, force all women to dress like Holly Hobbie, engage in sex with underage girls, and use inbreeding to spread fumaric aciduria.

Even stripped of these outrageous elements, Mormonism was still founded by a treasure-hunting charlatan, and still magically changes its holy doctrine every time the political winds change. Even stripped of these outrageous elements, then, Mormonism is false.

RELIGIONS POPULAR WITH FLAKEY CALIFORNIANS AND REBELLIOUS TEENAGERS

Jediism is false

Except for five-year-olds and certain adults with the mental capacity of five-year-olds, you will not meet many people who believe that the movie *Star Wars* is an accurate depiction of our universe. You will not meet many people who believe lightsabers actually exist. You will not meet many people who believe that there is some kind of universal power that radiates through us all (except, of course, for the Power of Love, which is able to make one man weep, to make another man sing, and to change a hawk to a little white dove). And you will certainly not meet many people who believe that the most powerful being in the universe is a Frank-Oz-voiced muppet incapable even of mastering English grammar at a junior-high-school level.

Nonetheless, George Lucas fans have campaigned repeatedly for Jediism to be accepted as an official religion. Toward this end, they pointed out the Jedi distinction between a dark side and a light side, the vows of celibacy forced (often with little success) on aspiring Jedi Knights, the rigid top-down hierarchy of the Jedi council, and the systematic indoctrination of young believers in the Jedi way. Given these arguments (and the fact that Jediism's claims are not substantially more outrageous than those of traditional religions), Great Britain has indeed added Jediism as one of the official state-sanctioned religions. In the 2001 U.K. Census, almost 400,000 people self-identified as Jedi Knights. Nonetheless, if it is not perfectly obvious to you that Jediism is false, you need more help than this book can provide.

Thelema is false

In the early 20th century the poet and mountaineer Aleister Crowley imagined that an entity named Aiwass ("the minister of Hoor-paar-kraat") dictated to him *The Book of the Law*. In it he asserted the three-part Law of Thelema:

1. Do what thou wilt shall be the whole of the Law.

2. Love is the law, love under will.

3. There is no Law beyond Do what thou wilt.

It is not difficult to see that the third part is the same as the first part, and that the second part contradicts them both. This fundamental illogic made it easy for Crowley to build a religion around these laws. The name "Thelema" is actually the transliteration of a Greek word meaning either "will," "intention," or "Geena Davis." Its followers are called Thelemites, after a disgusting brown food paste made from leftover brewers' yeast.

Thelemites worship ancient Egyptian gods like Had (the Secret Seed) and Nut (the Secret Nut) and Horus (the Secret Falcon), mostly due to Crowley's bizarre obsession with mummies. They also worship Harpo Marx, whom they consider the "god of silence."

Magick

Many Thelemites practice *Magick*, which Crowley defined as "the Science and Art of causing Change to occur in conformity with Will." (Another key Thelema practice seems to be blatant Disregard for the usual Rules of Capitalization.) At the time, critics complained that Crowley was merely reappropriating the well-known (and false) idea of *magic*; however, Crowley insisted that they were not the least bit similar:

Magick	Magic
contains the letter k	does not contain the letter k
applies even to mundane things like balancing a checkbook	applies only to non-mundane things like passing a hoop over a floating lady
requires invoking one's Holy Guardian Angel	requires invoking Blackstone
considers pen, ink, and paper to be magickal weapons	considers only vorpal weapons magical
promotes travel via "astral projection"	promotes travel via "floo powder"
canonical reference *Magick Without Tears*	canonical reference *Mindfreak: Secret Revelations*
fake	fake

"There ain't no Thelema here!"

Crowley died in 1947, but not before putting a curse on his doctor, who died a few minutes later. Today's Thelemites promote his teachings through religious practices that include yoga, keeping a diary, and listening to the Red Hot Chili Peppers album *Blood Sugar Sex Magic*. Thelemites band together in magical orders like *Argenteum Astrum* and *Ordo Templi Orientis*, where they learn things like the formula of the Rosy Cross, perfect control of the astral plane, and anal intercourse techniques.

However, there is no such thing as magick, anal intercourse techniques can be readily learned from videos on the internet, and Wilt Chamberlain (the most famous of all Wilts) is a horrible role model. Thelema is false.

55

Vodou is false

Vodou is a combination of African tribal religions and Catholicism that is popular in Haiti. (Louisiana Voodoo, Brazilian Candomblé, Cuban Santería, American Hoodoo, and Spanish Macarena are all similar enough to Vodou not to merit their own chapters.)

Vodouisants worship Bondyè, a polyester-resin-based putty manufactured by the 3M company, who (the putty, not the company) is believed to ignore them. For this reason, Vodouisants direct their prayers to Loa, who are either Catholic saints (according to Catholics), African spirits (according to Africans), or mutants with the ability to swim through solid matter (according to some Voudisants I met at Comic-Con).

During Vodou ceremonies, practitioners often dance around until they become "possessed" by individual Loa. Curiously, gay men are statistically more likely to be possessed by female Loa, which Vodouisants like to offer as evidence that homosexuality is neither biological nor environmental but is instead supernatural.

Zombies and Voodoo dolls

Vodou is best known in popular culture for its practices of creating Zombies (beings that are externally indistinguishable from normal humans but that lack "qualia") and of sticking pins in Voodoo dolls. This is an unfortunate misconception, as Vodou actually has little to do with Voodoo dolls, which are mostly made in China. (The zombie part actually is true and is the most likely explanation for the extreme unpopularity among Vodouisants of zombie-killing games like *Resident Evil*, *Doom*, *House of the Dead*, and *Little Red Riding Hood's Zombie BBQ*.)

Although Vodou features prominently in video games and "X-Files" episodes and James Bond movies, it does not have many well-known practitioners. The two most famous are probably the faux-Jamaican Miss Cleo, whose once-ubiquitous television commercials promised psychic advice for only 99 cents per minute (compared to the competition's $4.99

rates), and former WWE superstar Papa Shango, who once used his Vodou powers to make the Ultimate Warrior vomit green slime.

It turns out, however, that Miss Cleo is actually a Californian fraudster, and that Papa Shango is actually a pimp known as God the Father. Furthermore, many very smart philosophers argue that there are no such things as qualia, and that therefore zombies cannot possibly exist. Finally, the only actual Loa is a volcano that forms the bulk of the Big Island of Hawai'i, and that (mostly on account of its intermittent lava flows) is not a proper object of worship. Vodou, then, is false.

56

Wicca is false

After thousands of years of being drowned, burned at the stake, defenestrated, crushed by tornado-carried houses, and melted by farmgirl-thrown buckets of water, the witches and warlocks of the world in the 1950's hired a team of consultants who advised them to rebrand their beliefs as Wicca.

Wiccans worship both a horned god and a moon goddess, whose sarcastic insults and threats of violence toward each other were (according to Wiccan legends) the inspiration for "The Honeymooners."

"Such an ancient pitch"

Wiccans are most famous for believing that they can work magic. As stupid and unfounded as this belief is, it has been responsible for a huge quantity of beloved, witch-themed popular culture, including Andrew Fleming's *The Craft*, the 1971 Coven album *Witchcraft Destroys Minds And Reaps Souls*, "Bewitched" (the Dick York version, but not the Dick Sargent version, and certainly not the Nicole Kidman version), the *Worst Witch* books, Melissa Joan Hart's "Sabrina the Teenage Witch," the Steve Miller Band's hit song "Abracadabra," the WB's "Charmed," the *Harry Potter* books, Frank Sinatra's "Witchcraft," and the cult classic 1991 movie *Warlock*.

According to the fourth season of "Buffy the Vampire Slayer," witches tend to be lesbians, although the *American Pie* movies suggest that this is not the complete story.

The craft

Wiccans typically gather together in clay ovens known as "covens," in groups of exactly thirteen led by both a High Priest and High Priestess (who are typically married, but may also be part of a polyamorous triad). Wiccan rituals often involve pentacles (card games involving a 48-card deck), wands (spurring the now-famous debate "does the wizard choose the wand or the wand choose the wizard?"), athames (knives that are not for cutting but may only be used to "direct energy"), and chalices (cups that are considered a representation of the moon goddess's womb, and that you probably don't want to know what they use for). Wiccan rituals are often conducted in the nude ("skyclad"), mostly because it is very difficult to find Utilikilts that fit the large number of Wiccans with waist sizes greater than 60 inches.

Wiccans adopt craft names like Starhawk and Silver RavenWold and Mark Twain, either for symbolic purposes, so that their friends and employers won't be able to identify them with their postings on alt.religion.wicca, or because no one would take seriously a witch with a name like Samuel or Jenine.

But since there is no such thing as magic, since the only knives capable of directing energy are Ginzu knives, and since Utilikilts are severely unfashionable, Wicca is false.

57

Environmentalism is false

Although humans have worshipped various incarnations of the earth-goddess Gaia for centuries, modern Environmentalism was founded by Rachel Carson in 1962 with the publication of her book *Silent Spring*. Carson taught that the use of certain pesticides made Gaia unhappy, and that humans should simply accept the possibility of death from mosquito-transmitted malaria, a disease created by Gaia herself. Following closely behind her was prophet Paul Ehrlich, who preached that Gaia demanded the cessation of economic growth and human reproduction or else she would starve to death hundreds of millions of people.

The modern-day leader of the Gaia-worshippers is former vice president Al Gore, whose Nobel-Peace-Prize-winning film *An Inconvenient Truth* argues that long-term climate cycles represent Gaia's displeasure over a variety of carbon-dioxide-generating activities, and that we can appease her only by adopting radically ascetic lifestyles using "green" technologies conveniently provided by the investment firm he chairs.

Modern Environmentalists engage in a variety of seemingly-bizarre expressions of Gaia-praise:

- ritual inspection, sorting, and selective re-use of trash
- showering in the dark (or not at all)
- automobile non-ownership
- occupying trees to prevent them from being chopped down and turned into useful things
- consumption of more-expensive "organic" fruits and vegetables and dish soap
- limiting oneself to one square of toilet paper per movement
- composting
- firebombing university biology labs
- wearing pre-owned clothing
- smoking weed
- extreme self-righteousness regarding all of the above

Earth Day

The most important Environmentalist holiday is Earth Day, celebrated each April 22 to commemorate the birthday of Vladimir Lenin. (Although Lenin was not himself a Gaiaist, he nonetheless embodied Gaiaist values like anti-capitalism, persecuting and demonizing one's ideological opponents, and not tolerating dissent.) Environmentalists gather together each year to plant trees, make arts and crafts out of trash, and sing Earth Day songs like "I've Been Working on Recycling," "Care About Our Air," "This Old Earth," and "99 Bottles of Beer (In the Recycling Bin)."

Environmentalists also gather together at intermittent Earth Summits, where they fret about the possibility that indigenous peoples might be exposed to modern technology and healthcare, panic about greenhouse gases, and brainstorm ways to force people to ride public transit.

Kyoto

The holiest city for Environmentalists is Kyoto, the former capital of Imperial Japan, where in 1997 a number of countries agreed to appease Gaia by radically restricting emissions of greenhouse gases. Ever since, Environmentalists around the world have lobbied their governments to recognize and celebrate the importance of Kyoto. The United States, with a nominal tradition of "separation of church and state," has (at the time this book went to press) so far refused to ratify, although the Gaia-worshippers have been gaining political influence in recent years.

But there is no good reason to commemorate Lenin, used clothing spreads bedbugs, malaria is quite preventable, and the forecasts of Global Warming are based on the same methods of divination that predicted that semi-literate gardeners earning minimum wage would be reasonable candidates to repay half-million-dollar McMansion mortgages. Moreover, the earth is a space rock covered with water and trees and baseball diamonds, not a goddess named Gaia. Environmentalism is false.

58

New Age is false

New Age is a catchall term that refers to a variety of flakey religious behaviors. These behaviors have little in common except that they tend to be popular among hippies with names like Moonshadoe and Starfyre, are frequently promoted to gullible housewives by Oprah Winfrey, have tenuous connections to concepts from Eastern religions, are commonly advertised via handwritten flyers posted at organic co-ops, and don't actually do anything.

Harmonic Convergence

Many of the New Age practices have been around since the 1960s, but New Age really started thriving after the 1987 Harmonic Convergence, an event held at a variety of spiritually important "focus locations" like the Golden Gate Bridge, Disneyland, and Indiana. Participants engaged in a variety of bizarre rituals and prayers to bring about a period of "Earth cleansing," to which they credited the most important events of the next five years:

- Senate rejects nomination of Robert Bork to Supreme Court (1987)
- Introduction of Prozac (1987)
- Bush beats Dukakis (1988)
- Ayatollah Khomeini dies (1989)
- *Batman* revitalizes career of Michael Keaton (1989)
- First McDonalds opens in Moscow (1990)
- World Health Organization removes Homosexuality from list of Diseases (1990)
- Eastern Air Lines shuts down (1991)
- Exhumation of Zachary Taylor reveals no arsenic poisoning (1991)
- Pee Wee Herman arrested (1991)

Based on these and other similarly-impressive accomplishments, New Age ideas have steadily grown in popularity, and these days it is nearly impossible to flip through an issue of *Of Spirit* or *Infinite Healing* or *Think Well = Be Well Magazine* without encountering dozens of ads for "shaman this" and "energy that."

A sampling of New Age ideas

No list of New Age ideas can be wholly comprehensive, especially since they keep making up new ones every month. What follows should give you an idea of the breadth of New Age nonsense:

acupuncture: sticking needles into the human body to promote the proper flow of *qi* through "meridians"

alchemical divination: some combination of talking to spirits and transmuting lead into gold

alternative medicine: any "medical" practice for which there is no evidence of efficacy

astrology: see the "Astrology is false" chapter

aura: an invisible (yet colorful) field of radiation that surrounds a person and indicates his mood. Clairvoyants will gladly take your money and describe your aura to you, even though there is no evidence (other than the claims of clairvoyants) that auras exist. In fact, there is no evidence (other than the claims of clairvoyants) that clairvoyants exist!

channeling: communicating with spirits, including ghosts (which do not actually exist), angels (which do not actually exist), and whiskey (which does exist and is also tasty)

colon hydrotherapy: paying someone to squirt herbs and water up your ass, based on the ancient fear that there might be something "dirty" up there

crystals: are believed to have healing properties when placed on special "spiritually important" parts of the human body called "chakras"

divine energy healing: medicine based on the insight that all sickness and injury is ultimately caused by karmic damage to the soul

DNA activation: a process by which Indigos (and non-Indigos with "soul contracts") can (using "Keylontic Science") "activate" additional strands of their DNA to attain "higher dimensional awareness"

energy medicine: wearing magnetic jewelry endorsed by professional golfers

geomancy: predicting the future using dots

homeopathy: medicinal use of watered-down-beyond-recognition potions of non-medicinal herbs and spices

numerology: the belief in a mystical relationship between numbers and real-world events. Supposedly, 3 represents "perfection," 7 represents "perfection," 8 represents "perfection," and 57 represents "steak sauce."

psychics: people with abilities to predict the future. They are often employed by the police (to solve crimes), by marketers (to identify "the next big thing"), or by mortgage bankers (to assess borrowers' creditworthiness).

qi: see the "Feng Shui is false" chapter

reiki: by touching you inappropriately, a master can direct an intelligent "life force energy" to produce healing effects

shamanic healing: the use of rhythmic drumming to contact spiritual entities and ask for medical advice

soul retrieval: when part of your soul has been lost (perhaps on account of trauma or drunkenness), you can hire a shaman to go on a shamanic journey and find the missing pieces and "blow" them back into you

***The Secret*:** the Oprah-promoted (and demonstrably false) idea that, thanks to the "Law Of Attraction," you get whatever you wish for

vortex healing: a form of energetic therapy based on access to a vortex that connects our world with a healing energy realm

As not one of these ludicrous practices actually accomplishes what it claims to, New Age is false.

59

Astrology is false

Imagine you're talking to some girl at a party, and after a few minutes of conversation she decides that, on the basis of what she's learned about you so far, she's going to guess which month you were born in. "You're very witty, so I'm going to say 'August'." "Based on the number of times you've mentioned your ex-girlfriend you seem to have attachment issues, so were you born in April?" "You're boring me to death; is 'September' right?"

Of course this never happens (not just the girl talking to you at the party, but also the month-guessing) because it's perfectly obvious to everyone that how funny you are is determined not by which month you were born but instead by how cruel your parents (or the foster care system, or an abusive nanny) were to you at a very young age. And that people who were born in December actually have nothing universal in common, except perhaps getting screwed out of birthday presents on account of proximity to the gift-giving religious holidays.

Yet somehow, when we shift the dates forward by 20-ish days, the new, equally-ludicrous guesses are suddenly acceptable topics of conversation:

- "You were born between September 23 and October 23, and your boyfriend was born between April 20 and May 20? You two must be a perfect match!"

- "Really, you were born between December 22 and January 19? You don't seem like a December-22-to-January-19 birth!"

- "The newspaper advised that people born between May 21 and June 21 ought to 'let their natural powers radiate without interference' today, so that's what I'll be doing just as soon as I figure out what it means."

The positions of the stars and planets at the exact instant you were born, the astrologers claim, determine your temperament, your earning potential, your compatibility with the sorts of dating partners you'd meet in cheesy singles bars, and even your lucky numbers.

Signs of the Zodiac

As drawing up complete astrological charts would involve a lot of time and expense for something that doesn't even work, the typical astrologist focuses on his zodiac sign, a Latin cartoon character based on his birthday that determines his personality and life trajectory in the following manner:

Aries (The Ram): sometimes assertive and/or meek

Taurus (The Bull): sometimes assertive and/or meek

Gemini (The Twins): sometimes closed-minded and/or receptive to new ideas

Cancer (The Crab): sometimes assertive and/or meek

Leo (The Lion): sometimes closed-minded and/or receptive to new ideas

Virgo (The Virgin): likely to star in "Charles in Charge"

Libra (The Scales): sometimes closed-minded and/or receptive to new ideas

Scorpio (The Scorpion): sometimes closed-minded and/or receptive to new ideas

Sagittarius (The Archer): sometimes assertive and/or meek

Capricorn (The Sea-goat): sometimes assertive and/or meek

Aquarius (The Water Carrier): sometimes closed-minded and/or receptive to new ideas

Pisces (The Fishes): likely to take over father's Houston mega-church ministry

Case study: the Olsen twins

Being twins, *How the West was Fun* co-stars Mary-Kate and Ashley Olsen were born only minutes apart. And yet the pure, kind-hearted Ashley and the tormented, eating-disordered, rift-with-Paris-Hiltoned Mary-Kate could not be more different in character. What does astrology say about these differences?

Ashley Olsen	Mary-Kate Olsen
Born: June 13, 1986	Born: June 13, 1986
Became legal: June 13, 2004	Who cares?
Sexy	Yuck!
Sun Sign: Gemini	Sun Sign: Gemini
Moon Sign: Leo	Moon Sign: Leo
Ascendant: Aries	Ascendant: Aries
Horoscope: fickle, superficial, self-interested	Horoscope: charming, upbeat, witty
Actually: charming, upbeat, witty	Actually: fickle, superficial, self-interested
Verdict: Astrology is false!	Verdict: Astrology is false!

60

Objectivism is false

I know what you're thinking: Ayn Rand's philosophy of Objectivism is not a religion; it's an explicitly atheistic system of philosophy. And the fact that you are thinking that means that you didn't spend your junior year of college living with Pete DeWitt, who read *Atlas Shrugged* over winter break and returned for spring semester full of some kind of holy spirit, proselytizing "the virtues of selfishness" and "the morality of free market capitalism" and "the aesthetics of man qua man." It means you didn't have to accidentally read preachy newsletters from the Institute for Ayn-Rand-ian Studies when you were digging through piles of mail, looking for a birthday card from Grandma that you were pretty sure had a twenty-dollar bill in it. It means that your dining room was never stuffed full of boxes of *Anthem* that some wealthy industrialist had donated so that Pete could (whenever he got around to it) hand them out in front of the student union between classes. And it definitely means that you didn't have to listen to Pete, every time he came home drunk from partying with his ultimate frisbee team, slurringly complain how he would never find his "Dominique."

In fact, Objectivism's religious nature is quite apparent to anyone who reads all several-thousand pages of *The Fountainhead*; who takes thousands of dollars worth of classes from the Institute for Ayn-Rand-ian Studies; who participates in the periodic speed-dating events organized by aynHarmony.com; or who attends the various Rand-themed conferences held each summer, with talks like "Objectivism and the Future of First-Person-Shooter Video Games," "Ayn Rand's Conception of Girl-qua-Girl Pornography," and "The Physics of Selfishness."

To be fair, the Objectivists do have some good ideas, like withdrawing from the world and hiding out in the remote wilderness of Colorado to protest creeping collectivism, bravely opposing the removal of the word *I* from the English language, and blowing up buildings when their use betrays the architect's original intent. Nonetheless, their insistence that anyone who disagrees with them is "immoral" and "anti-human" and "anti-reason" and "anti-life" and "anti-Ayn" and "a meanie," their supernatural reverence for a dead screenwriter, and their ugly habit of excommunicating colleagues who doubt their dogma force us to treat them like every other religion. Furthermore, as most Objectivists live bitter, miserable existences in their parents' basements (hi, Pete!) where their only human contact is through Rand-fan websites, while many non-Objectivists lead extremely fulfilling lives ("but they only think their lives are fulfilling!"), Objectivism is quite clearly false.

Scientology is false

[At the insistence of my lawyers, portions of this chapter have been redacted.]

Once upon a time in Hollywood, being Jewish was the surest way to succeed in the entertainment industry. Jews like Metro, Goldwyn, Mayer, Warner, his brother, Steven Spielberg, Albert Brooks, and Elliot Gould ruled over the production houses like modern day Kings Solomon. But a couple of decades ago, this all started to change, and nowadays to get ahead in show business, you need to become a Scientologist.

Tom Cruise is perhaps the world's most famous Scientologist, but his partners-in-religion include "fat actress" Kirstie Alley, "loser" Beck, "Krippendorf's babe" Jenna Elfman, "human beatbox" Doug E. Fresh, Isaac "Chef" Hayes, Jason "His Name is Earl" Lee, "Natural Born Killer" Juliette Lewis, "Kurt-killer" Courtney Love, "Queen of Queens" Leah Remini, "Greased Lightning" John Travolta, and "musical albino" Edgar Winter.

Scientology was invented in the 1950's by science-fiction author L. Ron Hubbard. (Although Hubbard would frequently tell women he met in ▉▉▉▉ that the "L" was short for ▉▉▉▉, it actually stood for ▉▉▉▉▉.) Friends have speculated that Hubbard ▉▉▉ in order to ▉▉▉, although it is also possible he merely ▉▉▉ with ▉▉▉.

Unlike other religions, which tend to be eager to spread their doctrines, Scientology carefully meters out its teachings in expensive private lessons offered only to those devout enough to have provided in-case-of-apostasy blackmail material (one of the worst-kept secrets in Hollywood is that ▉▉▉▉ is secretly ▉▉▉ and once ▉▉▉ with ▉ in the ▉ after ▉▉▉). Typically they will set up a storefront or booth advertising ▉▉▉ or ▉▉▉ or even ▉▉ ▉▉. Once you step inside, they will ▉▉ you with an "e-meter," which is merely a ▉▉▉ similar to the one you built for a science project in the ▉▉ grade. They will next produce a report claiming that you have ▉▉▉ and that, unless you sign up for ▉▉▉

██████████, you will never be able to ██████, ██████, or ██████ to a woman. At this point, the training begins.

Most people, however, are not aspiring actors and therefore refuse to submit to this process. So unless you are a fan of "South Park" or the *Shaft* soundtrack, you may never have heard Hubbard's magical story. The Scientology creation story, which makes marginally less sense than most other religious stories, centers around an intergalactic ██████████ called Xenu. Many millions of years ago, Xenu feared being ██████, so he did what any other ██████████ would do. He used ████████████ to collect billions of his subjects, froze their souls using ██████████, flew them to earth (then known as "████████") in Douglas DC-8 aircraft, unloaded them around the bases of ██████████, and ██████████ a number of ██████████ ██████.

While this ██████ the billions of subjects, it left their thetans (what most religions would call "██████████") behind, at which point they were ██████████ and forced to watch movies (Scientologists disagree whether these were TBS "Movies for Guys who like Movies" or Lifetime "Estrogen Theater") which filled their heads with ██████ ██████. At this point the thetans flew off to cause ██████ sorts of ██████. If you are ill, Scientologists believe, or depressed or bored or sleepy, it is because thetans are ██████████ ██████ ██████ ██████. They will ██████ suggest that you ██████████, which (of course) is more likely to ████████████ than it is to ██████████ (unless you ██████ ██████ ██████, which never happens unless you're ██████ ██████ ██████████ or maybe ██████████████).

Famously, Scientologists do not believe in ██████████████ ██████, based on Hubbard's teachings that ██████ was merely caused by a ██████ of ██████████. Conveniently, this ██████ ██████████ millions of copies of *Dianetics* and *Scientology*, which ██████ ██████████ to the ██████ and hang around on the ██████ ██████ providing free ██████ for the ██████. Inconveniently, this means that when ██████████ ██ ██████ from ██████████ they often fail to ██████ ██████████, which sometimes leads to ██████ ██████, for example in the sad case of ██████ ██████ ██████, who is rumored to have suffered from ██████████, a condition that the church claims ██████ ██████.

At this point you're probably wondering how on earth anyone could ██████ ██████ ██████████. The answer, quite simply, is that ██████ will ██████ ██████ of anyone who even ██ to ██████. The cautionary tale of ██████ ██████, who (before her ██████ ██████) was a ██████ ██████ in ██████ ██████ provides clear demonstration that ██████████ ██████████ ██ ██████.

Some of Scientology's more bizarre practices include ██████████ ██████,

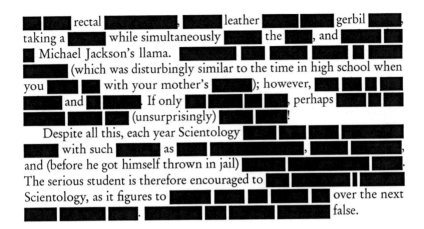

▮▮ rectal ▮▮▮, ▮▮ leather ▮▮▮ gerbil ▮▮, taking a ▮▮ while simultaneously ▮▮ the ▮▮, and ▮▮▮ ▮ Michael Jackson's llama. ▮▮▮ ▮ ▮▮ ▮ ▮ ▮▮ (which was disturbingly similar to the time in high school when you ▮▮ with your mother's ▮▮); however, ▮ ▮ ▮ ▮ ▮▮ and ▮ ▮▮. If only ▮ ▮ ▮▮, perhaps ▮▮ ▮ ▮ ▮▮ ▮ ▮ (unsurprisingly) ▮▮ ▮▮!

Despite all this, each year Scientology ▮▮ ▮ ▮ ▮▮ ▮▮ with such ▮▮ as ▮ ▮▮▮, ▮▮▮, and (before he got himself thrown in jail) ▮▮ ▮ ▮▮. The serious student is therefore encouraged to ▮▮ ▮ ▮ ▮▮ Scientology, as it figures to ▮▮ ▮ ▮ ▮ ▮ over the next ▮▮ ▮▮ ▮. ▮▮ ▮ ▮ ▮▮ false.

62

Other cults are false

A cult is a set of beliefs and practices, often centered upon specific supernatural and moral claims about reality, the cosmos, and human nature,
and often codified as prayer, ritual, and religious law. Cults also encompass
ancestral or cultural traditions, writings, history, and mythology, as well
as personal faith and mystic experience. The term "cult" refers to both
the personal practices related to communal faith and to group rituals and
communication stemming from shared conviction.

It is not difficult to notice that the definition of *cult* is quite similar
to our definition of *religion*. There are, however, important differences
between the two:

religion	cult
uses psychological coercion to recruit and retain members	uses psychological coercion to recruit and retain members
"us versus them" mentality	"us versus them" mentality
criticism met with threats and legal action	criticism met with threats and legal action
promises extra-earthly rewards for followers	promises extra-earthly rewards for followers
frowns on interactions with non-members	frowns on interactions with non-members
often many hundreds of years old	rarely many hundreds of years old

If you were to start your own religion (perhaps in order to make
money or to acquire a collection of underage wives), chances are it would
be dismissed as a cult for several decades or longer. Even traditional
religions like Scientology and Falun Gong were once considered cults,

over the strong objections of the all-knowing and all-powerful L. Ron Hubbard and Li Hongzhi.

A sampling of cults

An even moderately comprehensive listing of cults would take up many books of its own. Please do not take the omission of *your* cult from this chapter as evidence of its non-falseness. If it's not listed here, that simply means that in addition to being false, it's not very important and not very interesting.

Amway

Recruits its members, euphemistically known as "Amway Business Owners," into participating in pyramid-ish multi-level marketing schemes selling cleaning products, make-up, and health supplements.

Art of Living

Teaches that medical treatments can efficaciously be replaced with a combination of breathing, listening to tapes of Guru Sri Sri Ravi Shankar's voice, and standing outside Indian groceries recruiting new members to attend his seminars.

Aum Shinrikyo

Launched a sarin gas attack on the Tokyo subway to overthrow the Japanese government, to discourage the use of public transit, and to stimulate sales of Japanese cars, with the ultimate goal of installing founder Shoko Asahara as king of Japan.

Bhagwan Shree Rajneesh

Contaminated several Oregon salad bars with salmonella in 1984 to incapacitate voters and help themselves win local elections.

Branch Davidians

Lost shooting war with Janet Reno in Waco, Texas.

Cargo Cults

Build mock airstrips and coconut radios to summon cargo-carrying World War II planes to return.

Eckankar

Emphasizes "soul travel" to commune with ECK Masters like Fubbi Quantz (the spiritual guide for Christopher Columbus), Rebazar Tarzs (who is over five hundred years old and lives in a hut), and Rami Nuri (who guards the Temple of Golden Wisdom in Retz, the capital of Venus).

Hare Krishna

Shave their heads and chant mantras in airports.

Heaven's Gate

Added suffix "-ody" to adopted names, underwent castration to "avoid the urges," and committed mass suicide to celebrate the arrival of comet Hale-Bopp.

LaRouchians

Aggressively recruit college students to advocate for a "New Bretton Woods" system of fixed currency exchange rates and to persecute musicians who use "incorrect" tunings.

Manson Family

Believed that the Beatles' *White Album* was full of hidden messages directed at them, murdered actress Sharon Tate, wrote horrible songs.

Movementarians

Live in a compound, waiting for The Leader to open the doors of "The Forbidden Barn" and lead them to the planet Blisstonia.

NXIVM

Also known as "The Purple Pill™ That Offers 24-Hour Heartburn Relief," insists that followers refer to its founder as "Vanguard" and its president as "Prefect."

Order of the Solar Temple

Stockpiled weapons then committed mass-suicide in 1994 (possibly in response to Newt Gingrich's "Contract With America").

People's Temple

Promoted Marxism, hung out with Harvey Milk, moved to Guyana, murdered Congressman Leo Ryan, drank poisoned Kool-Aid.

Raëlians

Believe that all life on earth was created by space aliens known as Elohim; always attempting to clone things.

Scientology

Is now featured in its own chapter ("Scientology is false"), after having successfully made the cult-to-religion transition in late 2003.

Thuggees

Led by the villainous Mola Ram, used the blood of Kali to brainwash followers.

Transcendental Meditation

Promote world peace through "yogic flying."

Trekkies

Worship fictional space commanders Kirk, Picard, and (rarely) Janeway.

U-Men

Use mutant body parts to gain superhuman powers.

Unification Church

Worship Sun Myung Moon as "savior, messiah, and returning lord," hold mass weddings (and mass honeymoons) with pairings chosen by church leaders, communicate with spirits of the dead.

RELIGIONS THAT WERE MADE UP VERY RECENTLY

63

Intelligent Design is false

Anyone who learns even a tiny bit of evolutionary biology realizes that the biblical creation story represents the fantasies of a pre-literate people unnaturally obsessed with fruit and snakes and the naked human body, not a believable description of the origins of man. In order to prevent children from realizing this almost-common-sense fact, religious types have often tried to suppress the teaching of evolution, replacing the relevant chapters in biology classes with Bible lessons. Predictably, many students and parents and teachers and potential employers object to the replacement of science with topics that not only are not science but also are false.

This is the sort of conflict that led to the famous Scopes Monkey Trial, indelibly captured in the Pulitzer-Prize-winning drama *The Diary of Anne Frank*. John Scopes, charged with violating Tennessee's anti-evolution Butler Act, was crucified on the famous "cross of gold" by Bible expert and also-ran Presidential candidate William Jennings Bryan. Unless you grew up in Alabama or Tennessee or Georgia, you probably saw the movie version in seventh grade one day when your teacher was too hung-over to lecture.

Although the law was eventually overturned on account of being wildly unconstitutional, in recent years supporters of biblical creationism have recast their arguments in the guise of a pseudoscience called Intelligent Design.

The argument from design

Intelligent Design is at its core a rehash of William Paley's eighteenth-century teleological argument, or "argument from design," for the existence of god:

(a.) If I found a watch on the beach, it would have to have a designer.

(b.) I found a watch on the beach.

(c.) It's not yours? It must be god's, then.

These days watches don't have designers but are instead made by the Japanese, and Paley's argument is even less convincing than it used to be.

The argument from Intelligent Design

Nonetheless, in the last twenty years an ambitious crowd of theologians and faux-scientists has reworked the argument using scientific-sounding language:

(a.) In certain biological structures, if you remove one piece the whole thing breaks.
(b.) For instance, if you remove a human's heart, she will stop working.
(c.) Therefore there's no way that evolution could have produced a human.
(d.) If something wasn't produced by evolution, it must have been designed by an intelligence.
(e.) Hence, there must be some intelligent creature that designed humans.
(f.) Although I will never say so in public, when speaking to Jewish audiences I will insist that this intelligent creature is the Jewish god, when speaking to Christian audiences the Christian god, and when speaking to Zoroastrian audiences the Zoroastrian god.
(g.) Please don't ask me why the same argument doesn't imply that some super-god created god, some super-super-god created super-god, and so on.

Teaching the controversy

A few members of the Intelligent Design crowd strategically pretended to believe in biology just long enough to get credentialed as scientists, and they have used these credentials to successfully lobby a number of school boards to "teach the scientific controversy" in biology classes. In order to defray accusations that they are religiously motivated, these scientists support a number of other pseudo-scientific controversies:

- Despite claims to the contrary by Apollo astronauts, might the moon actually be made of green cheese?
- Although there is no evidence for their existence, could orgones be the cause of cancer?
- Even though pranksters have admitted creating them, could crop circles be the work of aliens?
- Are the yeti and sasquatch related, or is their similar appearance and behavior just coincidence?

- Could the water shortages faced by the developing world be solved through dowsing?

Along similar lines, there is a push in many states to give teachers the so-called "academic freedom" to teach their classes as they best see fit. I am not unsympathetic to this point of view, as my (very brief) stint as a high school history teacher was marred by continual struggles over my academic freedom to teach things as varied as "the Civil War was fought not over slavery but rather over a woman," "the purported 'moon landing' actually took place on a sound stage in Studio City, California," and "American foreign policy post-9/11 is being controlled behind the scenes by blood-drinking reptilian humanoids from Alpha Draconis." However, in this case it doesn't make sense, as evolution ought to be a perfectly uncontroversial theory.

The basic ideas underlying evolutionary theory

1. Parents tend to have kids who are biologically similar to them. Tall people tend to have tall babies. Chinese people tend to have Chinese babies. Ugly people tend to have ugly babies. The wicked tend to have wicked babies. Starfish tend to have starfish babies.
2. Occasionally, mutations occur. These are usually harmful but on rare occasions are useful. For instance, occasionally someone will be born with six fingers on one of his hands, and when I finally find this six-fingered man I intend to tell him, "Hello. My name is Inigo Montoya. You killed my father. Prepare to die." Similarly, it sometimes happens that a cheerleader is born with exceptional healing abilities, or that a Canadian comes into the world with an adamantine skeleton and metal claws that can spring out and retract from his hands.
3. People (or creatures) who are better at surviving and reproducing will have on average more descendants than people (or creatures) who stink at either surviving (e.g. daredevils) or reproducing (e.g. nuns).

As you can see, each of these is basically common sense; the theory is itself controversial only because it contradicts the millennia-old creation myths of semi-literate cave people, which (despite their obvious fictional nature) are still cherished today. The overwhelming evidence is that design is utterly unintelligent, demonstrating that Intelligent Design is false.

64

Falun Gong is false

Falun Gong (or Falun Dafa) is a Chinese religion founded in 1992, as a response to (depending on whom you believe) the founding of the European Union, the release of Microsoft Windows 3.1, the opening of Euro Disney, the death of Friedrich Hayek, or the ratification of the Twenty-seventh Amendment. Li Hongzhi, the founder, is supposed to have acquired supernatural powers while studying with (depending on whom you believe) a Taoist master, a Buddhist monk, a Communist philosopher, a Korean pop star, Bill Cosby and Mortimer Ichabod Marker, or Stanley Kaplan.

Zhuan Falun

The basic teachings of Falun Gong are set out in the book *Zhuan Falun* ("Dianetics"), which was for many years the bestselling book in China, until finally displaced by the charmingly unauthorized *Harry Potter and Leopard-Walk-Up-to-Dragon*. Since I don't expect you to actually read the book, I have collected a handful of online-bookstore reviews that should give you some idea of what it's like:

> By "A Customer": The author scientifically explains supernatural powers gained during cultivation (e.g. the histological base of celestial eyes is pineal gland and what is the difference between Qigong and physical exercise), and he also adds new meaning into reincarnation. Through many times of reading of Zhuan Falun, I have realized that Zhuan Falun is the greatest book and a scripture of extensive knowledge and profound scholarship in the history of the cycle of mankind. Carrying the book w/ you, on your person, supposedly protects you from accidents. Zhuan Falun cannot be analysed as it is not a book of theories, but the truths of the universe. Be guided by your own heart, not others.

By "Not the same person as A Customer": The author scientifically explains supernatural powers gained during cultivation (e.g. the histological base of celestial eyes is pineal gland and what is the difference between Qigong and physical exercise), and he also adds new meaning into reincarnation. Through many times of reading of Zhuan Falun, I have realized that Zhuan Falun is the greatest book and a scripture of extensive knowledge and profound scholarship in the history of the cycle of mankind. Carrying the book w/ you, on your person, supposedly protects you from accidents. Zhuan Falun cannot be analysed as it is not a book of theories, but the truths of the universe. Be guided by your own heart, not others.

By "Falun Gong is not a Cult, All Praise to Li Hongzhi": The author scientifically explains supernatural powers gained during cultivation (e.g. the histological base of celestial eyes is pineal gland and what is the difference between Qigong and physical exercise), and he also adds new meaning into reincarnation. Through many times of reading of Zhuan Falun, I have realized that Zhuan Falun is the greatest book and a scripture of extensive knowledge and profound scholarship in the history of the cycle of mankind. Carrying the book w/ you, on your person, supposedly protects you from accidents. Zhuan Falun cannot be analysed as it is not a book of theories, but the truths of the universe. Be guided by your own heart, not others.

Alien Plots

Besides lecturing people about his supernatural powers, Master Li teaches that mixed-race people are part of an alien plot to convince humans to abandon their (racially-pure) gods, and that these same aliens have perfected cloning technology with the ultimate goal of replacing humans. Li also teaches that homosexuality is "disgusting." Falun Gongers try to live according to the motto "Don't Think. Just recite the Master's teaching," which they then use as an excuse to explain their poor performance on "Jeopardy."

The Chinese government has many times attempted to crack down on the practice of Falun Gong, and (depending on whether you believe the government-controlled Chinese media or Falun-Gong-controlled websites) either Gongers have been setting themselves on fire in protest, or the Chinese government has been setting Gongers on fire in protest. Similarly, either Gongers have graciously donated thousands of organs to the needy, or the Chinese government has been forcibly harvesting organs from imprisoned Gongers and selling them to politically-connected cirrhotics. If, like me, you consider both sources untrustworthy, you are forced to conclude that probably both versions are true.

Truthfulness, compassion, forbearance

The three primary values of Falun Gong are truthfulness (sometimes translated as "truthiness"), compassion (sometimes translated as "kindness"), and forbearance (a type of loan-forgiveness). One result is that Falun Gongers make terrible mortgage brokers, and largely managed to avoid the housing bubble.

The practice of Falun Gong consists mostly of a handful of stretching exercises with names like Buddha Stretching a Thousand Arms, Buddha Kicking a Thousand Asses, Falun Cosmic Cogs, Falun Spacely Sprockets, Reinforcing Supernatural Powers, and Negative Reinforcement of Subnatural Powers. These exercises are designed to rotate the falun, a spinning ball of energy located in the abdomen, and to absorb energy from the universe.

However, there is no spinning falun in most people's abdomens, Buddha never kicked even a single ass, and Li Hongzhi has no powers, supernatural or otherwise. Falun Gong is false.

65

Choprism is false

While most people from India speak incomprehensibly (if you attended college you probably had such a person as a teaching assistant for your math courses), occasionally you will find one who speaks with a rich, beautiful, British-style accent. For reasons that are unclear but that probably have to do with the movie *Indiana Jones and the Temple of Doom*, many people find these well-spoken Indians unrealistically credible. This, as far as I can tell, is the only explanation for the popularity of Deepak Chopra. (It still leaves as a mystery the popularity of Dr. Phil.)

Deepak Chopra originally trained as a medical doctor in India. After establishing legitimate credentials, he promptly began to preach (and sell) an incoherent mishmash of Buddhism, Western medicine, Ayurveda (a pre-scientific folk medicine based around massage therapy and heavy-metal-laden herbal compounds), quantum mechanics, homeopathy, meditation, belief in the paranormal, yogic flying, and intelligent design. Despite (or perhaps because of) its nonsensicality, Choprism has grown startlingly popular with well-educated liberals.

Accordingly, Chopra's incoherent rantings about spirituality have become a staple of PBS pledge drives. The following "thank you gift" schedule is pretty typical:

- At the $50 level: ethically made Deepak Chopra T-shirt, exquisitely manufactured by monks using renewable green energy generated from wind and solar power.
- At the $100 level: Paperback copy of *Unlocking the Third Jesus's Seven Hidden Dimensions of Spiritual Success.*
- At the $250 level: Chopra Center Aromatherapy Blend 3-Pack (for Pitta, Kapha, and Vata mind-body types).
- At the $500 level: Personalized tutorial explaining how to get the *Journal of the American Medical Association* to publish an article promoting your company's goods and services.
- At the $1000 level: Ugly red glasses.

Additionally, Chopra is often invited to post poorly-argued exposi-
tions of the Choprist religion on otherwise-unreligious left-wing websites
(whereas your author's well-argued debunkings of religion are only ever
invited to appear in hand-mimeographed 'zines distributed in anarchist
bookstores in San Francisco). "You're Going to Like The Way You
Look...I Guarantee It" entrepreneur George Zimmer recruited Chopra
to serve on the Men's Wearhouse board of directors (despite Chopra's
cultivated-to-appear-eccentric fashion sense). And Chopra has been able
to open a self-themed luxury spa offering multi-thousand-dollar Choprist-
propaganda weekends with names like "Perfect Healing," "Soul of Healing," "Journey in Healing," "Sensual Healing," "Quantum Healing," and
"Expensive Meditation Lessons for the Gullible."

But as PBS is well-known for promoting untruths (including the
existence of magic school buses, giant talking birds, and Spider-man), as
yogics can't actually fly, and as all of Deepak's "spiritual" ideas are just the
sorts of nonsense we've debunked in other chapters, Choprism is false.

66

Rastafari is false

Rastafari is based on the belief that Haile Selassie I, emperor of Ethiopia from 1930 to 1974, was (along with Jesus) an incarnation of god. As Rastas do not believe that god can die, they insist that Selassie's 1975 "death" was in fact a hoax, and that he is actually in hiding with Elvis Presley, living on a diet of peanut-butter-and-banana sandwiches, ham-bone dumplings, and bacon-fried corn. Rastafari is most popular in Jamaica, but all over the world small communities of pot-smokers have adopted Rasta practices.

(You may have heard the Rasta religion described as Rastafarianism. Rastas themselves find this word offensive, as their religion involves "rejecting all -isms, even jism." Fortunately for the Rastas, my desire to offend them is outweighed by my desire not to type any more than absolutely necessary.)

Rasta religious ceremonies include Reasoning (a time when everyone smokes weed and eats Fritos and pretends to be profound before collapsing into fits of giggling), Grounation (a time when everyone smokes weed and eats Fritos and pretends to be profound before collapsing into fits of giggling), and Up in Smoke (a time when everyone smokes weed and eats Fritos and watches Cheech and Chong movies before collapsing into fits of giggling).

How high

As you may have gleaned by now, marijuana is very important to the practice of Rastafari, where it is known by such names as ganja, herb, healing of the nation, mary jane, puff, rainy day woman, santa maria, grass, bud, reefer, cheeba, schwagg, chronic, crazy weed, dagga, dinkie dow, kate bush, and wacky tobaccky. Along similar lines, Rastas enjoy reggae music, which makes them (along with Orthodox Jews) pretty much the only ones.

Most Rastas have seen *The Matrix* movies too many times and believe that the world is divided into the holy land of Zion (i.e. Africa) and the corrupt "matrix" of Babylon (i.e. everywhere that's not Africa). In order to confuse "agents," Rastas frequently replace the "you" and "me" sounds in words with "I," resulting in linguistic abominations like "Inity," "Inuch," "ITube," "Electric Ith," "Ianspirited," "Idicine," "Ilancholy," "Ilodrama," "Isothelioma," and "Inopause."

Although on multiple occasions Selassie offered that he was "fully human" (and hence could not be god), Rastas tend to overlook this by insisting (mostly based on a misunderstanding of what the word "fully" means) that he was both "fully human" and "fully divine."

Anyway, Haile Selassie is dead (and certainly is not god). Therefore Rastafari is false, although I suspect it will continue to be popular for as long as marijuana-smoking remains legal.

67

Đại Đạo Tam Kỳ Phô Độ is false

Đại Đạo Tam Kỳ Phô Độ ("Great Religion Third Period Revelation Salvation"), or Caodaism (as those of us who don't have all those crazy characters on our keyboards prefer to call it), is practiced by millions of people in Vietnam, and a few hundred people not in Vietnam.

Caodaism considers itself the "Third Alliance between God and Man." Caodaists are demure about what the first two might be, though most scholars suspect they were the Anglo-Portuguese Alliance and the Alliance to End Hulkamania. Caodaists believe that there are 72 planets with intelligent life, and that earth is the 68th-closest to heaven. (The four further-away planets are supposedly Planet of the Apes, Klendathu, Cybertron, and Hoth.)

The Caodaists worship Cao Dai (Hightower from the popular *Police Academy* series of movies), who is supposed to have exposed himself to a civil servant named His Venerableness Ngô Van Chiêu in the early 20th century. God revealed himself in Vietnam, Chiêu argued, because of his love of the tripe soup phộ and of bánh mì sandwiches.

Caodaists are unusual in that they worship a number of different-religion saints, including Victor Hugo (who wrote *Les Misérables*), Descartes (who persuaded the philosophy community that he existed), Louis Pasteur (who created the first vaccine for rabies), and Vladimir Lenin (who launched the Red Terror to arrest and execute "enemies of the revolution").

The practice of Caodaism involves séances, ouija boards, the basket-with-beak technique, seer stones, lampadomancy, lecanomancy, libanomancy, cromniomancy, crithomancy, and the use of a large, vibrating egg. Caodaists are also required to sign up for special meal plans, which range from six vegetarian meals a month to "all you can eat soup and salad bar."

The center of Caodaist worship is the Holy See temple at Tay Ninh, which – in a fit of jealousy over the relative popularity of Catholicism – Caodaists stocked with their own Pope, Cardinals and Bishops. (I am still waiting for them to hold their own Cadaver Synod.) There they teach the fundamental principles of Caodaism, including the Universal Family, the Following of the Way, and the Existence of the Spirit World, all with the goal of achieving freedom from the cycle of birth and death.

Two one-time events, however, cannot form a cycle; the basket-with-beak technique has never worked any time I've tried it; Lenin was no saint; and the Drake Equation shows that there are certainly not 72 planets with intelligent life. Caodaism is false.

68

Cheondoism is false

Admit it, you've never heard of Cheondoism. You probably suspect I'm making it up, which is why I encourage you to visit your local library and find some books on it. I particularly recommend *Cheondoism: The Religion I'm Not Making Up!*, *Chondogyo: The Religion of the Cosmos That Blossomed in Korea*, and Eugene O'Neill's masterpiece *Donghak Becomes Cheondoism*.

Cheondoism is practiced by a handful of South Koreans and is also the only non-Juche religion allowed in North Korea. Cheondos worship Haneullim, an old-timey Korean sky god repackaged by the monk Choe Je-u in his famous "Twenty-One Character Incantation":

> *Chi-keui Keum-chi won-wi Tai-dang*
> *Si Chun-chu Cho-hwa Chung*
> *Yung-sei Pool-mang Man-sa Chi*

Roughly translated, this means

> Choe Je-u made up a religion
> Based on the worship of Haneullim
> Please don't execute him for heresy.

Shortly afterward, Choe Je-u was executed for heresy, probably because he wrote his rhyme in nonsense syllables and no one at the time was able to understand it.

For a description of its goals, I defer to the terrifically lucid Cheondoist website chondogyo.or.kr:

> the ultimate religious aim of Chondogyo is to establish heaven or paradise on earth in which all people enjoy equality and freedom in a return to the origin and become one society and a return to the origin and become one world erected by transcendent sages on earth bearing the heart and mind of God.

Like the gods of so many other religions, Haneullim is conveniently both inconceivable and indescribable. (If you ever want to mess with a Cheondoist, you might try pointing out to him that "inconceivable" is itself a description.) Haneullim is supposed to live inside you, and (according to his followers) is responsible for the kim chee cravings you sometimes develop late at night.

Devout Cheondists promote values like "having the right spiritual force" (which mostly entails avoiding the fictitious spiritual forces that arise from non-inertial spiritual reference frames), "maintaining a steadfast heart and mind" (usually by limiting intake of bad cholesterol), and "living in absolute perfect unison with the one vast living organism of the cosmos" (which is believed to be Pando, a 107-acre clonal colony of Quaking Aspens in Utah).

Cheondoists are less forthcoming with the specific details of their religious observances. What we can say is that important practices include Ch'ongsu (water filtration), Shimko (swearing in Korean), and Chumun (repeating Choe Je-u's sacred incantation).

In addition, Cheondoists celebrate major holidays like Foundation Day (in remembrance of when Hari Seldon's image appeared in the Time Vault), Earth Day (which they appropriated from the Environmentalists), Man Day ("a day that we men stand together as a united front to take part in strictly man things"), and Commute Another Way Day (when you can win fabulous prizes if you take the bus to work).

But there is no Haneullim, the cosmos is not a vast living organism, and nothing that co-exists with Juche could possibly be true. Cheondoism is false.

69

Clapton-worship is false

This chapter has a certain poignancy for me, as I have only seen two of this book's would-be gods live in concert from fifth-row seats that I woke up early on a Saturday morning in tenth grade and sat in the lottery line outside Ticketmaster for four hours in order to purchase, and Eric Clapton is one of them.

The following facts are not in dispute: First, Clapton was born in 1945 in England. Second, Clapton was ranked fourth in Rolling Stone's "100 Greatest Guitarists of All Time" list. (Serious Clapton-worshippers still grumble that Duane Allman should never have been ranked above him.) And third, Clapton briefly dated singer/songwriter Sheryl Crow in the mid-1990's. While each of these is an admirable achievement, very few people would ascribe Clapton supernatural powers on their basis.

But for a small subset of diehard fans, Clapton is god, as can be seen from the oft-photographed graffiti that appeared, image-of-Virgin-Mary-like, on a subway wall in England in the 1960's. While anyone with even the tiniest bit of common sense would attribute this graffiti to hooligans, a minority of music fans (possibly high on "Cocaine") took this mysterious writing as proof of Clapton's divinity.

Don't get me wrong, "After Midnight" is a pretty good song, especially the part where it goes "gonna shake your tambourine." And Clapton at least had the good sense to date Sheryl Crow before she embarked on her bizarre "one toilet paper square per poo" crusade. Nonetheless, an even semi-omniscient god would have the good sense not to record a cover version of the unlistenable "I Shot the Sheriff." Clapton-worship, then, is false.

70

Dungeons and Dragons is false

Dungeons and Dragons, invented in 1974 by Gary Gygax and Dave Arneson, is a syncretism of Greek Mythology, the fantasy world of ultra-Catholic J.R.R. Tolkien, Thelema, and Yahtzee. Its adherents, known as gamers, have few official places of worship, but often gather together in college dorms or in someone's basement. Admitted celebrity gamers include Mike Myers, Stephen Colbert, Vin Diesel, and Robin Williams. Due to a history of persecution, many followers of Dungeons and Dragons keep their interest secret, so there are probably many more celebrity gamers we'll never know about.

While most other religions insist on certain strict rules for being good, gamers are allowed to choose a life of good, neutrality, or evil, and can subsequently devote themselves to worshipping an appropriate god chosen from the *Players Handbook*. Popular choices include Wee Jas (goddess of vanity), Hugh Jas (god of gluttony), Garl Glittergold (god of humor), Gary Glitter (god of child pornography), Boccob (god of magic), Kobbob (god of skewered meat), Hobnob (god of kibitzing), and LOLth (goddess of cat macros).

Just as Hindus and New Age believers make up stories about past lives, gamers create themselves mystical fantasy personae like elven wizards and half-orc barbarians and gnomish druids, adopting mystical fantasy names like Cruneiros Spiritforged the Whitesmith and Gurhana Lorearthen the Drover and Yorelij Innis the False.

Adventuring

Spiritual leaders known as Dungeon Masters spend years studying the arcane *Dungeon Master's Guide*, after which they are qualified to lead gamers through imaginary (but licensed and authorized and professionally illustrated) adventures, often using tiny, hand-painted, pewter relics. There are hundreds of official adventures; the following are some of the most popular:

- Expedition to the Ruins of WTC Seven
- The Conspiracy to Bring Down WTC Seven
- The Dragons of WTC Seven
- Return to the Ruins of WTC Seven
- Lost Song of the Lizard King
- Pyramid of the Louvre
- Ghost Dad
- The Hidden Island of Cuba
- Temple of the Dog / Hunger Strike (double adventure)
- Vegetables of the Green Giant
- Against the Cult of the Sci-Fi Author
- MILF Hunt

New media

Dungeons and Dragons leapt in popularity in the 1980s following the success of its eponymous Saturday morning cartoon featuring "Charles in Charge" co-star (and "BibleMan" star) Willie Aames, and today its ritual polyhedral dice are rolled all over the world. Over the years, gamers have (as tributes to their various gods) slaughtered millions of imaginary orcs, half-orcs, quarter-orcs, trolls, half-trolls, silver dragons, platinum dragons, Rearden-Metal dragons, fire giants, water giants, were-wolves, were-tigers, were-rats, were-frogs, were-sheep, zombies, vampires, vampire zombies, liches, half-liches, demi-liches, hemi-liches, semi-liches, arch-liches, and de-liches.

With the advent of computerized pseudo-random number generators and the internet, many gamers have converted to pay-by-the-month online imitations like *World of Warcraft* and *City of Herpes* and *MoneyQuest*. Yet while these faddish cults fade in and out of style, the original Dungeons and Dragons religion retains its core of devoted followers. While most other religions modify their rules as rarely as possible and only when forced into it, the high priests of Dungeons and Dragons recreate their entire canon on a surprisingly frequent basis, creating new gods, changing the rules of battle, eliminating character classes, and (most importantly) producing costly new versions of the canonical manuals and guides and handbooks that players have to purchase to keep adventuring.

However, there are no such things as orcs or paladins or gnomes or trolls or bags of holding or potions of jump. There's no "handbook" for life (other than this book, of course). And no amount of dice rolling could possibly save you in the unlikely event you were hit by a magic missile, touched by a cockatrice, or zapped with a rod of cancellation. Dungeons and Dragons, then, is false.

71

Singularitarianism is false

Unless you are the sort of nerd who hangs out at comic book conventions, who celebrates Captain Kirk's birthday (March 22, 2233), and who invented your own computer programming language, you are probably not familiar with singularitarianism (also sometimes called extropianism, transhumanism, futurism, and botulism). Singularitarianism refers to worship of the singularity, a Twilight-Zone-ish other dimension that lies behind a door that you unlock with your mind, and that represents a world so different from ours that (except for those of us who are Science Fiction authors) we are incapable of imagining it. (Being incapable of imagining it doesn't seem to stop singularitarians from believing in it.)

Theories of the singularity

Fortunately for us, a variety of authors have proposed dumbed-down versions of the singularity that are simple enough that I can understand them and explain them to you:

- Eventually toasters will become so intelligent that they will begin adjusting their own settings and eventually take over the world. (Vernor Vinge)
- Solar-powered computers will eventually trap humans in a simulated reality so they can use us as an energy source. (Larry and Andy Wachowski)
- "When I was a kid, there was only one channel on TV, and then there were five, and then fifty, and now there are thousands of channels, and if technology keeps accelerating at this rate there will soon be infinitely many channels!" (Ray Kurzweil)
- The computer network we've built to run our defense systems will eventually become self-aware and attempt to eradicate mankind by sending robots backward in time to carry out strategic assassinations. (James Cameron)

- Nano-robots will replicate and consume all matter on earth, turning everything into a tasty, grey, high-protein goo. (Eric Drexler)
- If we freeze our brains after we die, in the future smart people will figure out how to bring us back to life and will give us a job working for one of their interplanetary delivery companies (Benjamin Franklin / Matt Groening)

Of course, these are all predictions about the future, which makes it impossible to demonstrate definitively that they will never happen. Nonetheless, the main argument in favor of them (besides misleading graphs) seems to be that they appear as plot points in science fiction stories. Accordingly, you would be equally well-served pinning your religious hopes on the Hugo-award winning prediction that the war simulations you participate in as part of Battle School represent actual battles fought against Formics, that you will someday be able to form a line marriage on the moon, or that some day the new mathematics of psychohistory will enable large-scale prediction of the future. Until the Singularity arrives, Singularitarianism is false.

Hooliganism is false

If you are American, you are probably familiar with soccer, the cute little "run and kick and don't touch the ball with your hands" game played primarily by uncoordinated 5-year-olds wearing awkwardly oversized shin-guards and knee-pads. What you may not know is that in most other parts of the world this same game is called "football," is played by adults, and is even more popular than Ultimate Fighting Championship.

Football partisans cheer for and diligently follow the progress of clubs named after their home cities and/or weapon-storage facilities, like "Manchester United" and "Arsenal" and "Tottenham Gun Locker." Many times these supporters are not merely fans but are actually hooligans, which means that they support their club with vandalism, racist taunts, fist-fights, rock-fights, gun-fights, bottle-fights, and girl-fights directed against the hooligans of rival teams.

The few historically-minded hooligans like to trace their traditions back to the Nika riots of 532, where fans of the rival Blue and Green chariot-racing teams, possibly angry over a disputed yellow flag, brawled out of the Constantinople Hippodrome, threw rocks at police cars, killed tens of thousands of people, attempted to overthrow the emperor Justinian, looted Korean groceries, and destroyed half the city. Most historians, however, consider modern hooliganism an outgrowth of the deadly British "Mods versus Rockers" wars of the 1960s.

Modern hooligans gather together in "firms" like Yid Army, Dick Armey, Subway Army, Orkin Army, and Huddersfield Young Casuals, which organize fights against rival firms, deliver death threats to star players of opposing teams, and sacrifice burnt offerings like cars and trash cans and stadium seats to hooligan gods like Diadora, Umbro, and Kelme.

Hooliganism remains popular as (like so many other religions) it appeals to many of the baser human instincts like violence and revenge and contempt of socialist ideology. However, as there is no evidence that these fights and sacrifices accomplish anything other than landing hooligans in hospitals and jail, hooliganism is false.

Juche is false

Throughout history, unscrupulous political leaders have noticed the success with which religious leaders have acquired absolute power, and have accordingly tried to recast their ideologies in religious terms.

German ruler Adolf Hitler turned his National Socialism into a "positive Christianity" based on Aryanism (the notion that white Germans were a "master race"), Blümchenkaffee (moderation in caffeine intake), Führerprinzip (absolute obedience to a hierarchy of "naturally superior" leaders), Fahrvergnügen (what makes a car a Volkswagen), Volksgemainshaft (state control of arts, media, education, and community), Gleichschaltung (the elimination of individualism), Verkehrsausscheidungsziffer (long-distance telephony), and anti-semitism (Jew-hatred).

Similarly, communist leaders Joseph Stalin and Mao Zedong both created cults of personality around themselves, using their control of all aspects of the state to present themselves as god-like and infallible, to bed nubile supermodels, to install reverential portraits of themselves in private homes and public places, to send people who had made fun of them in middle school off to Siberian labor camps, to require their subjects to create works of literature and art and music praising them, and to get preferential access to tickets for popular Olympic events.

Since the deaths of Hitler and Stalin and Mao, Hitlerism and Stalinism and Maoism have pretty much faded away, remaining popular only with a handful of skinheads in Idaho, the president of Venezuela, and the proprietors and clientele of a Chinese restaurant in Venice, California.

North Korea

Not wanting to leave a void, North Korean Eternal President Kim Il-Sung established a similar religious ideology with his 1955 speech catchily-titled "On Eliminating Dogmatism and Formalism and Establishing Juche in Ideological Work." The practical details of Juche can be found most clearly in current dictator and *Team America: World Police* star Kim Jong-Il's *On the Juche Idea*:

Chajusong: the achievement of a "true freedom" unknown in the west, characterized primarily by strict obedience to one's government and state control of the media

Songun: the forced diversion of resources away from frivolous pursuits like eating and shelter and healthcare toward more important causes like militarism and repression

Kimjongilism: (formerly Kimilsungism) reverence of Kim Jong-Il, including posting pictures of him in every household, voting him (despite his diminutive stature and poor free-throw shooting) for the NKBA "Sixth Man Award" every year, and routinely choosing him as *Korean People* magazine's "Sexiest Dictator Alive"

Kangsong Taeguk: a strong and prosperous state, based on a policy of economic self-reliance, kidnappings, and starvation

To demonstrate the strength of Juche, North Korea has built a Juche Tower in Pyongyang, which is perpetually illuminated using the bulk of the poor country's scarce electricity. Each April 15, to celebrate Kim Il-Sung's birthday, Juche believers celebrate the Grand Mass Gymnastics and Artistic Performance Arirang, where thousands of schoolchildren make mosaics out of colored cards to demonstrate just how disciplined they can be.

In the 1990's, as the result of either Songun or Kangsong Taeguk (or perhaps both), the North Korean economy entered a state of extreme stagnation, characterized by famine and terrible poverty. Out of this grew the new Juche doctrine of "One meal a day should be more than enough for anyone" and the new Juche prayer of "Please, god or Kim Il-Sung or anyone, send us food!" Thanks to these religious innovations, it is estimated that no more than 600,000 Koreans died of starvation.

But as the practice of Juche has produced poverty rather than prosperity, as Kim Jong-Il is certainly not a god, and as eating is much more important than repression, Juche is false.

74

Pastafarianism is false

After existing in secrecy for hundreds of years, the Church of the Flying Spaghetti Monster revealed itself to the public in 2005. Its practitioners, commonly known as Pastafarians, surfaced to demand that the Kansas school board debating the inclusion of Intelligent Design in its science curriculum also include the Pastafarian theory that the world was created by an all-powerful Flying Spaghetti Monster.

Pastafarians claim that the FSM is invisible and undetectable by science, although they also claim (incongruously) that he looks like a clump of tangled spaghetti with two eyestalks and two meatballs and an indeterminate number of "noodly appendages." Their theology asserts that the FSM created the universe after drinking heavily, after which he planted false evidence for evolution in order to test Pastafarians' faith. Just like the Judeo-Christian god, the FSM is also believed to have created the world in seven days, albeit on an accelerated schedule involving three days of rest and a "midgit" [sic].

The Pastafarians' main religious text is *The Gospel of the Flying Spaghetti Monster*, supposedly dictated by the FSM to a pirate. This gospel contains eight "I'd really rather you didn'ts," covering everything from dietary restrictions to sexual conduct. Adherence to the didn'ts is supposed to qualify dead Pastafarians for their heaven, which they believe contains a multitude of "beer volcanoes" and a "stripper factory."

Part of me suspects that Pastafarianism is not a serious religion but was designed primarily to mock some of the more prominent religions. On the other hand, this suspicion is rooted primarily in the ridiculousness of the notion of a Flying Spaghetti Monster. Using this sort of ridiculousness as a criterion I could just as easily mount the same suspicion against any of the other religions in this book. As I have first-hand experience that those other ridiculous religions are practiced in earnest, I am forced to assume that the same is true of Pastafarianism, and I am forced to point out that Pastafarianism is (like every other kind of food-worship) false.

RELIGIONS THAT ARE BARELY RELIGIONS BUT ARE STILL RELIGION ENOUGH TO BE FALSE

Deism is false

Deism is the belief that some sort of god created the universe, at which point he promptly went on vacation (possibly to Sea World) and was never heard from again. Although it is not such a popular religion today, Benjamin Franklin's "Almanack of chicken foup for the Deist's foulle" was the bestselling pamphlet of both 1773 and 1774, and John Philip Souza's "Deist Nuuuts" sold more piano rolls in the 1890's than any other religious song. There are a few different justifications for Deism, although the following is typical:

> It's pretty damn implausible that there's a god who sometimes meddles in our world but was willing to sit by idly and allow Marilyn Monroe's candle to burn out long before her legend ever did; however, there's no way to offer evidence against the god-created-the-world-then-checked-out assertion (even though that assertion adds nothing to our understanding of the how the world works or how best to live our lives), and by comfortably "believing" in this absentee god, I can avoid being called an atheist, which would severely hamper my ability to join the Boy Scouts, be elected President, found the University of Virginia, fly a kite during a lightning storm, or chop down a cherry tree.

As the Boy Scouts are nowadays considered severely uncool (and as Virginia currently has more than enough universities), this type of justification is these days much less compelling, and Deism has experienced a steep drop-off in popularity. Nonetheless, just in case it experiences some sort of revival, it is worth pointing out that there is not even a tiny shred of evidence for Ben Franklin's god, and that Deism is false.

Unitarian Universalism is false

There comes a time in every religious person's life when he begins to suspect that his religion is false. (Often that time is when he reads this book.) Most frequently he speaks with his pastor or imam or witch doctor, receives a platitude or movie quote along the lines of "a faith which does not doubt is a dead faith" or "doubt isn't the opposite of faith; it's an element of faith" or "I find your lack of faith disturbing," promptly ignores his reservations, and returns to the fold. In rare cases he abandons his religion altogether; in very rare cases he writes a book encouraging others to do the same. And most of the rest of the time, he converts to Unitarianism, the un-religion.

The purple dinosaur

Unitarians follow the "I love you / you love me" teachings of Barney the Purple Dinosaur. Rather than wasting time on long and boring holy books or complicated divine revelation, Unitarianism expresses its kindergarten-level theology in the form of alternate lyrics to the Rodgers and Hammerstein song "Do-Re-Mi":

> One, each person is worthwhile
> Two, be kind in all you do
> Three, we help each other learn
> Four, and search for what is true
> Five, all people need a vote
> Six, work for a peaceful world
> Seven, we care for Earth's lifeboat
> That will bring us back to me and UU!

Who are the Unitarians?

Because of their core value of noncommitment, Unitarians include atheists, monotheists, bitheists, tritheists, tetratheists, hexatheists, heptatheists, octatheists, enneatheists, decatheists, hendecatheists, dodecatheists, icosatheists, centatheists, chiliatheists, myriatheists, polytheists, and pantheists.

In a recent survey, Unitarians were asked to choose descriptions of their beliefs. The following were the most common answers (responders could pick more than one):

- humanist: 33%
- inhumanist: 24%
- spineless: 47%
- Christian, sort of: 15%
- Christian, but not really: 13%
- Christian, but one of the good ones: 10%
- JuBu: 19%
- earth-centered: 38%
- moon-centered: 24%
- chocolate-centered: 19%
- Buddhist: 15%
- fat Buddhist: 8%
- pagan: 16%
- fat pagan: 16%
- atheist: 17%
- pantheist: 8%
- enneatheist: 4%
- Sunkist: 25%

As you can see, Unitarianism does not actually make any claims about the world, and therefore it is not so much false as it is useless (unless you are a teacher at a hippie pre-school, in which case it could serve as the basis for an emergency syllabus).

77

Pantheism is false

Pantheism is the belief that everything is god. That's right, everything. Here is a (necessarily) incomplete list of Pantheist gods:

John "Bluto" Blutarsky ● Menander I ● Alexander the Great ● Ramkhamhaeng the Great ● Narai The Great ● Olaf the Troll God ● Hugh the Great ● Gustavus Adolphus the Great ● Otis Day ● *Grand Theft Auto 3* ● Louis the Great ● Doug Neidermeyer ● Buddha Yodfa Chulaloke the Great ● The episode of "Home Improvement" where the family finds out Randy might have cancer ● Wilhelm the Great ● Yahweh ● Elvis Presley ● Pompey the Great ● Miracle Whip ● Earle Combs ● St. Leo the Great ● Jasmine ● Gero I the Great of Marca Geronis ● George Pipgras ● Yak Milk ● Cool Whip ● Satana ● Shapur the Great ● Dean Vernon Wormer ● Jim Morrison ● Marion Wormer ● Lachit Borphukan ● Louis the Great ● Nader Shah the Great ● Camel Urine ● The Osborn's Key Mouse ● Toshiro Takashi ● Dinza ● Tamburlaine the Great ● *War and Peace* ● Eric "Otter" Stratton ● Cigarettes ● Rajendra Chola The Great Tamil King of India ● Spanish Flu ● Lamar Latrell ● Anthony the Great ● Fred "The Ogre" Palowakski ● The Easy-Bake Oven ● Bhumibol Adulyadej the Great ● Adolf Hitler ● Disco Stu ● Stan Gable ● Joe Dugan ● the fractional quantum Hall effect ● Limp Bizkit ● Alfred the Great of Wessex ● Bob Meusel ● Boodog ● Coach Harris ● Malaria ● Waite Hoyt ● Gertrude the Great of Helfta ● Hanno the Great ● The Green Death ● Gwanggaeto the Great of Goguryeo ● Glorificus ● Hopkinsville Community College ● Ashoka the Great ● Mandy Pepperidge ● Sancho III the Great ● Spanish Fly ● Johnny Grabowski ● Theodoric the Great ● Polio ● Wilcy Moore ● St. Nicholas the Great ● Julie Wera ● Tony Lazzeri ● Frederick the Great ● Bayinnaung the Great ● Simeon I the Great ● Jesus Christ ● Gilbert Lowell ● Rosie O'Donnell's blog ● Alexis Arquette ● William I the Great ● Batman ● George "Goober" Lindsey ● Antiochus the Great ● The Powers That Be ● St. Basil the Great ● Pu Zoramthanga ● Tiridates the Great ● The 1971 ICF Canoe Sprint World Championships ● Betty Childs ● Zits ● Ray Morehart ● Polish blackened death metal band Behemoth ● Maggot Cheese ● Vytautas the Great ● Soft-boiled Fetal Duck ● Louis Skolnick ● Abbas the Great ● Stinkor ● Eudes-Henry the Great ● Lou Gehrig ● Naresuan The Great ● Sejong the Great ● Kamehameha the Great ● Casimir the Great ● Krishnadevaraya the Great ● Despot John Palaeologus ● the painting *Washington Crossing the Delaware* ● Alaska Route 10 ● Amarapuri ● Valdemar I the Great ● Xwida ● Harshavardhana ● Yu the Great ● Mithridates the Great ● Prokop the Great ● Grand Duchess Anastasia ● Taksin the Great ● Arnold Poindexter ● Llywelyn the Great ● Smallpox ● Mubarak Al-Sabah the Great ● Mark Koenig ● Poa annua ● Moctezuma the Great ● Dirty Sanchez ● Cyrus the Great ● Herod the Great ● Dutch Ruether ● Larry "Pinto" Kroger ● Vladimir the Great ● Small Seal Script ● Justinian the Great ● Nicholas II of Russia ● Bob Barker ● The Hall of Presidents ● the singer from Toad the Wet Sprocket ● Mayor Carmine DePasto ● Shivaji the Great of India ● Mithridates the Great ● Bird Flu ● Jesse James ● Kangxi the Great Emperor ● Velveeta ● Danny Burke ● The Love Boat ● Peter the Great ● Chandragupta Maurya ● Myles Thomas ● Chuck Barris ● Sargon the Great ● The Red Death ● Dudley "Booger" Dawson ● Alain I the Great ● Theobald the Great ● Cholera ● Charles the Great ● Robert Hoover ● Andy Kaufman ● Herb Pennock ● Ramon Berenguer III the Great ● Judy ● Theodosius the Great ● Ubu Roi the Dog ● Shia LaBeouf ● Rek ● The Country Bear Jamboree ● Photius the Great ● Ben Paschal ● The University of Santo Tomas Symphony Orchestra ● 7263 Takayamada ● Lice ● Pacal the Great ● Darius the Great ● Daniel Simpson "D-Day" Day ● Cedric Durst ● Mata Nui the Great Spirit ● Askia the Great ● AIDS ● Matteo Rosso the Great ● Joe Giard ● Harold Wormser ● Dean Ulich ● Catherine the Great ● Tupac Shakur ● Boils ● Napoleon the Great ● Kent "Flounder" Dorfman ● Canute the Great ● Rajaraja The Great ● Herpes ● Chulalongkorn the Great ● Donald "Boon" Schoenstein ● Mike Gazella ● a sloop of war in the United States Navy during the American Civil War ● Pat Collins ● Benny Bengough ● Anawrahta the Great ● Ferdinand the Great ● Mstislav the Great ● Hemorrhoids ● Conrad the Great ● Petar Kresimir IV the Great ● Xerxes the Great ● First Evil ● Karim Khan the Great ● Urban Shocker ● William the Great ● Akbar the Great ● The 1917 St. Louis Browns season ● Jangsu The Great ● Illyria ● St. Macarius the Great ● Meiji the Great ● Sergeant Slaughter ● Ramesses the Great ● Constantine the Great ● Ebola ● St. Gregory the Great ● Rhodri the Great ● Greg Marmalard ● The Black Death ● Umar the Great ● Alfonso the Great of León ● Watford Grammar School for Girls ● Babe Ruth ● the Spanish Civil War ● Parakramabahu the Great ● George V of the United Kingdom ● Otto I the Great ● the WOPR supercomputer in the movie *WarGames* ● Tigranes the Great ● that soiled back-issue of *Juggs* you found in the woods ● Jon Bauman

I could continue, but any religion that posits Jon Bauman as a god is obviously false.

78

Agnosticism is false

If you hang out in secular circles (which, for some reason, are never perfectly round), you are likely to meet a not-insignificant number of people who self-identify as agnostic, which is a polite way of advertising that they have no idea what they believe. There are two common strains of agnosticism: "I'm not sure whether god exists" and "it's impossible to know whether god exists (and therefore I'm not sure whether god exists)."

The second form is plainly untrue: when the face of Jesus appears as streaks on a newly (but poorly) washed window, this provides (very, very meager) evidence for the Christian god's existence. Similarly, the major parties' choices of candidates for the last several Presidential elections provides powerful evidence against the existence of a benevolent, all-powerful god. Neither of these constitutes 100% proof, but (unless you are some sort of pipe-smoking, black-turtleneck-wearing philosophy professor) 100% proof is never a prerequisite for belief in anything. We believe that the sun is going to rise tomorrow, that dropped toast will always land buttered-side down, that it was that weird payroll analyst from the third floor who scratched our new Hyundai in the parking lot, and that the muscular, oddly-tattooed plumber will always drop his pants and violate Jenna Jameson as soon as the "boom-chicka-wow-wow" music starts, even though we cannot prove any of these things.

Clearly, then, it is possible to form a belief as to whether a god or gods exist. The remaining agnostics would have you believe that they either choose not to or are personally unable to form such a belief. And yet a moment's thought reveals this position to be equally nonsensical. Christianity claims that accepting Jesus as one's savior is a necessary condition to avoid an eternity of being tortured by a devil who can't even manage to win a fiddle competition. Allah mandates fasting from sun-up to sundown throughout the month of Ramadan. Yahweh forbids the wearing of wool-linen blends. When agnostics avoid kneeling down for Jesus's approval, gorge themselves year-round at the all-you-can-eat Indian lunch buffet, or buy whatever is on sale at Old Navy without first scrutinizing the contains-ingredients tag, they are necessarily demonstrating implicit beliefs about the truth of Christianity, of Islam, and of Judaism.

If you pressure her, an agnostic will usually admit that in fact she disbelieves in Zeus, in Make-make, in Nyambe, and in Ahura Mazda. (If you pressure her more, she might go on a date with you, although it will likely be a wishy-washy, non-committal, I'm-not-sure-if-I-want-to-hold-your-hand, maybe-we-should-just-be-friends kind of date.) For reasons that have never been made quite clear, she will be less likely to admit strict disbelief in Jesus or Yahweh or Allah or Aphrodite. Eventually she may withdraw to her incoherent last refuge: "I'm not religious; I'm spiritual."

"Non-religious spirituality" is false

More than twenty percent of the girls in my daily emails from Match.com identify themselves as "spiritual but not religious." If you are not a member of this group, you are probably right now thinking to yourself, "aren't spiritual and religious the same thing?" Indeed they are; however, some religious people are ashamed of being religious (as well they should be) and have instead adopted a form of politically-correct self-denial. (These are the same people who insist that we call the short "vertically-challenged," the stupid "learning-disabled," the unfunny "differently-humored," and prison schools for wicked kids "alternative education.")

People who make this distinction often seem to use religion to mean "organized religion" and spirituality to mean "unorganized religion." So if you believe in Jesus because the man in the funny outfit at church told you to, that's "religion"; if you believe in Jesus because it makes you feel all warm and funny inside to do so, that's "spirituality." The non-religiously spiritual offer a variety of defenses of their faith:

- "There are many paths to the truth."
- "It is important to find your own way to god (or not)."
- "There's got to be something more out there, there's just got to."
- "Church is boring, but I'm scared of death."
- "I believe in a faith that taps into the spirit that's already there."
- "You're probably right that my religion is false, but I'd rather not think about it."
- "I am a mushy-headed non-thinker."

These weak-spined commitment-phobes are half-correct, in that there are indeed many paths. But, as we have seen throughout this book, each of these paths leads to a set of false beliefs, and falsely claiming to be "not religious" can't change this fact. What's more, as they won't actually admit belief in anything, their religion is too flimsy to disprove. (Which, to them, is a point of pride.)

Apatheism is false

Apatheists don't particularly care whether your religion is true or false; they consider the question not worth worrying about. As I have gone to the trouble of writing this book, it should be clear that I disagree with them.

Imagine that one of your friends comes over to visit and claims, "by the way, there's a man with a gun out in the street, shooting people who look at him strangely." One reasonable response might be disbelief (especially if your friend is Ashton Kutcher), another might be to call the police. However, a clearly unreasonable response would be "I don't care whether such a shooter is out there or not; it's not worth worrying about."

Given how many of the major religions promise torture and unhappiness and punishment to non-believers, only the most pain-loving masochists could believe that "which religion is true?" is an unimportant question. It is quite possibly the most important question there is, which means I have done you an incredible service in writing this book. Don't you forget it! (I accept both cash and personal checks. No credit cards, please.)

ODDS AND ENDS

"What about my religion?"

There is a slight possibility that, despite the all-encompassing nature of the preceding chapters, I have somehow managed not to mention your religion. In all likelihood this is because you made it up yourself (in which case the chapter on Clapton-worship should mostly apply) or because it is only practiced by a few hundred of your closest relatives in a small desert town on the border of Colorado and Arizona (in which case the chapters on Mormonism and "Other Cults" should take care of you). If you consider yourself a Pagan, then the chapters on Wicca and Unitarian Universalism should be all you need. Perhaps your religion is mostly premised on the otherwise-illegal use of the psychoactive decoction *ayahuasca*, in which case the chapter on Rastafari applies. If you are a Mennonite, the chapters on Amishness and Quakerism should be sufficient to debunk your beliefs. It might be that you consider yourself a Discordian who believes that "chaos is all there is" or a Satanist who espouses a life of self-indulgence, in which case you should probably read the chapters on Thelema, Objectivism, and Pantheism. Maybe you practice Xiantianism, a combination of Buddhism, Taoism, Confucianism, Christianity, and Islam, in which case I recommend you read the chapters on Buddhism, Taoism, Confucianism, Christianity, and Islam (at which point you might as well just read the whole book).

If there is an underlying theme in this book, it is not merely that your religion is false, but that your religion is false in just the same ways that every other religion is false. That you should see yourself reflected in *every* chapter. That your god is just as implausible as all the gods that you already don't believe in. That your religious practices are just as outrageous and ineffective as everyone else's.

Moderation as a virtue?

Occasionally you will meet "Christians" who realize that the story of Jesus could not possibly be true; nonetheless, they will insist that he was a "great moral teacher" who deserves worship on that basis alone. If you are ever trapped at a cocktail party speaking with one of these pseudo-believers, it is probably a good idea not to ask her what the object of worshipping a dead teacher is, and it is probably an even better idea not to drunkenly assert that you worship would-be astronaut Christa McAuliffe for similar reasons. (Unless you want a permanently-staining, cherry-red girl-drink thrown all over you, in which case mock away.)

Similarly you can find Jews who selectively ignore the Bible's more odious commandments, Muslims who support terrorist bombings "but only if no one gets hurt too badly," Hindus who eat beef "as long as it's organically-raised and grass-fed," and Mormons who will drink coffee as long as it's not from Starbucks. "Look at us," it's as if they're saying, "we only believe in the good parts! We're not like those icky fundamentalists!"

Nonetheless, these moderate believers in false religions are equally deserving of our reprobation. Although they may reject a few of the most pernicious precepts of their religions, the ones they keep are still both abhorrent and false. The reform Jew who observes Passover is still celebrating a (fictional) genocide. The liberal Christian who suspects (solely on the basis that it makes her feel better) that "good-hearted" nonbelievers might possibly get to go to heaven despite their nonbelief still believes that there are some number of people who get punished for eternity partly because a (fictional) woman was convinced to eat a forbidden apple by a talking snake several thousand years ago. The moderate Muslim who only prays three times a day and only insists on facing vaguely in the direction of Mecca still is offering praise to a bloodthirsty, violence-loving fictional character.

Covering for extremists

What's worse, though, is that these moderates implicitly give cover to all the worst extremists. When Christian nuts picket gay funerals, when Jewish lunatics insist that traffic signals be reprogrammed to automatically give WALK signs on Saturdays, when hardcore Scientologists kidnap and brainwash their critics, when Muslim fundamentalists agitate for the overthrow of governments not based on Islamic principles, and when Rapa Nuians violate zoning laws to construct unsightly giant heads; the most damning, the most effective, the most obvious retort is that their religions are false. That god cannot hate gays, cannot care whether someone pushes buttons on the sabbath, cannot take issue with the principles underlying a government, and cannot be a giant stone head, because he is imaginary.

But that simple truth might offend these thin-skinned wimps, which leaves people in the position of having to argue "yes, Allah might want you to kill some people, but not these people," and "yes, Xenu might hate some thetans, but not those thetans," and "yes, Zeus might have fathered a lot of mortals, but not this mortal." In order not to step on any pseudo-religious toes, we're forced to implicitly grant the plausibility of the fundamentalists' fictional world.

Imagine that some television star (as is so often the case these past fifteen years, I am thinking of Laura Leighton, although you are free to imagine someone else if it helps) begins hearing voices in her head, commanding her to kill her fans. You and your moderate friends can argue over what the voices in her head "really" want her to do, but it would be much more practical (not to mention much less delusional) to point out that these voices are obviously hallucinations and to demand that she get medical help. Don't we owe our "talks-to-Jesus" acquaintances the same type of concerned honesty?

Non-overlapping magisteria?

In the late 1990's, well-known paleontologist Stephen Jay Gould contracted a nearly fatal case of non-overlapping magisteria from eating some pork that had spoiled. Seized by delirium, he produced the book *Rocks of Ages*, in which he advanced the idea that science and religion do not conflict whatsoever, as they are tools for investigating completely distinct sets of questions. Science, he argued, is a tool for explaining how the universe works, religion a tool for investigating "ultimate meaning" and "moral value."

Around the same time, the National Academy of Sciences (which sounds like one of those egghead private schools that rejected me for admission) put out a statement asserting that "science and religion occupy two separate realms of human experience. Demanding that they be combined detracts from the glory of each."

There are a couple of problems with this view. First "ultimate meaning" and "moral value" are examples of weasel phrases that in a religious context don't mean what they sound like. Pretty much every religion teaches that the ultimate meaning of life (as well as the highest moral value) is to follow its religious commandments. That is, Gould and the Academy are asserting that you should let witch doctors and shamans and priests tell you what to do, since they claim to know about moral values while science does not. And besides, using science to help make these kinds of decisions might diminish the witch doctors' glory.

A less misleading version of this assertion might then be that "religion is a way to surrender absolute authority over your behavior to ancient books and their power-hungry modern-day interpreters," although when phrased this way it sounds less complimentary.

The more damning criticism of this approach is that (as we've seen) almost every religion does attempt to explain how the universe works. Judaism and Christianity and Islam insist that the world was created in a six-day period less than ten-thousand years ago, and that the sun moves through holes in a dome-like firmament about the earth. Scientologists assert that a common ▆▆ ▆▆▆▆▆▆▆ allows "auditors" to examine your ▆▆▆ ▆▆▆. Intelligent Design believers argue that evolutionary biology is false. The Catholic Church spent decades persecuting scientists who dared suggest that the earth revolved around the sun. Hellenists imagine that people can be quickly and easily transformed into cows. Hindus believe that a human head could be seamlessly replaced with an elephant's head without any loss in mental capacity. Environmentalists claim that simple computer models can accurately predict the behavior of complex systems hundreds of years in the future.

Insofar as a religion makes absolute claims about the world (which, with the exception of Unitarianism, they all do), it is fundamentally in conflict with science, whose premise is that all claims about the world are subject to revision in the face of evidence. The only way that science and religion can avoid conflict is if one or both is completely neutered.

Isn't atheism a religion?

Although most people seem to enjoy learning about why other people's religions are false, very few of them seem to react positively to the news that their own religion is false. Sometimes their unhappy reactions involve childish name-calling, promises to pray for your soul, or eggs thrown at your new Subaru. Occasionally, people will respond (usually in a smug and mocking manner) that "atheism is a religion too."

Recall, if you can, our working definition of religion:

> A religion is a set of beliefs and practices, often centered upon specific supernatural and moral claims about reality, the cosmos, and human nature, and often codified as prayer, ritual, and religious law. Religion also encompasses ancestral or cultural traditions, writings, history, and mythology, as well as personal faith and mystic experience. The term "religion" refers to both the personal practices related to communal faith and to group rituals and communication stemming from shared conviction.

Atheism is a single belief ("your religion is false"), but consists of no practices, no supernatural claims, no moral claims, no prayers, no rituals, no religious laws, no ancestral traditions, no cultural traditions, no canonical writings (though this book seeks to change that), no history (except for general, non-religious world history), no mythology, no faith, and no mysticism.

If atheism were a religion, then other equally-common-sense beliefs like "Zeus doesn't exist" and "There's not a pink unicorn in my yard" and "*Your Religion is False* deserves a Pulitzer Prize" would necessarily be "religions" too. And an internet search quickly confirms that no one considers pink-unicorn-not-in-my-yardism a religion.

Occasionally you see quotes like "Atheism is a religion in the same way that not collecting stamps is a hobby." However, as not collecting stamps actually *is* one of my hobbies, I prefer my line of reasoning.

"But without religion..."

Some people argue that religion is a necessary source of morality, and that if people all realized their religions were false, they would no longer have any incentives to fly airplanes into skyscrapers, to chop off the tips of their babies' penises, to restrict poor people's access to contraception, to censor cartoons, to make it difficult to purchase liquor on Sundays, to stone homosexuals, or to murder apostates and heathens. Society, they argue, would subsequently break down.

Obviously the consequences of religious belief are quite independent of the truth thereof. This objection then boils down to the belief that "even if my religion is false, the world is a better place when people believe in it (and therefore I need to kill those who don't believe in it)." But is this even true?

Religious apologists tend to smugly point to Joseph Stalin, who was an atheist and who killed millions of people in the name of communism, "an atheistic philosophy." (These apologists tend to ignore that communism is merely an economic ideology; and that there are plenty of god-believing communists, many of whom insist that, for example, "Jesus preached that we should replace the dictatorship of the bourgeoisie with the dictatorship of the proletariat," or "Mohammed insisted that workers of all countries unite," or "Make-make demanded common ownership of the means of production.") It is certainly true that the Soviet Union was officially an atheistic state; however, as most of Stalin's victims were his political opponents, "because he was an atheist" seems much less compelling an explanation than "because he was a power-hungry dictator."

After all, the Nazis promoted a form of Christianity (and yet killed lots of people), Idi Amin was a Muslim (and yet killed lots of people), and religious terrorists are (in the name of one god or another) currently killing people all over the world. Moreover, there are plenty of non-religious people who lead pleasant, productive lives, never sending millions of their countrymen to death camps, never filling the Nile River with enough bodies to clog the Owen Falls Dam, and never blowing up nightclubs in Bali. In short, religious belief is neither a necessary condition nor a sufficient one for living a virtuous, non-genocidal life.

What the proponents of the "but without religion" argument seem to be implying is that only the threat of the sky-man's wrath keeps them from dishonoring their parents, starting an affair with your wife, coveting your house, bearing false witness against you, and killing you in your sleep. "If there is no god," they like to suggest, "then everything is permitted."

If you live near one of these "everything is permitted" religious mad-men, I suggest you invest in a good security system before he reads this book, realizes there is no Ahura Mazda, decides to ignore the community's (non-religious) disapprobation of and criminal penalties against burglary and murder, and tries to break into your house and kill you. On the other hand, if your neighbors are already non-religious, you're probably safe.

86

"What about all the good things religion did?"

Defenders of religion will often point out that religion has throughout history been responsible for any number of laudable accomplishments. For example, without religion, Saint Peter would never have built his beautiful basilica in Rome; Ford and Mercedes would never have designed state-of-the-art "popemobiles"; Leonardo da Vinci would never have painted *The Last Supper*; LaHaye and Jenkins would never have written *Desecration: Antichrist Takes the Throne*.

However, this sort of reasoning ignores Bastiatian "What is Seen and What is Not Seen" effects. In the absence of religion, Saint Peter might have designed an elegant shopping mall; Ford and Mercedes might have developed hydrogen cars or plug-in-hybrids or convertibles; Leonardo da Vinci could have spent more time creating bestselling codes and drawings of naked men in circles; LaHaye and Jenkins might have instead written a series of novels about a club of babysitters and their adventures.

Other defenders will point to "humanitarians" like Mother Theresa, who (on account of her belief in the Pope) selflessly tried to convince the poor of India that suffering (and, in particular, leprosy) was "a gift from god" and attempted to amend the Irish constitution to prohibit divorce. Like Al Gore, who (on account of his belief in Environmentalism) carries on an incessant quest to bring the world's economies to a halt and drive millions of people deeper into poverty. And like Muammar al-Gaddafi, who (as part of his devout Muslim beliefs) waited only 15 years before accepting responsibility for his country's bombing of Pan Am Flight 103 over Lockerbie, Scotland.

Yet again, it is impossible to definitively attribute these actions to religious views. Perhaps a non-religious Mother Theresa would have equally celebrated leprosy as "just plain good luck"; perhaps a non-religious Al Gore might merely express a heartfelt, secular preference for human suffering; perhaps a non-religious Gaddafi might have never had the plane blown up to start with. We have no way of knowing. Yet, as it is clear that equally good (if not better) things might have been done in the absence of religion, this objection is in the end pretty worthless.

87

"But religion is what gives my life meaning..."

Another common objection to the points raised in this book is that religion serves as a source of comfort or meaning or purpose for people. I have no doubt that this is indeed the case; however, serving as a source of comfort does not make a belief true. After all, the "Harry Potter" books serve as a great comfort to me (or at least they did until J.K. Rowling callously outed happily-in-the-closet headmaster Albus Dumbledore), but you will rarely find me arguing that Hogwarts School of Wizardry and Witchcraft is a real place, that use of the Avada Kedavra killing curse is actually unforgiveable, or that Quidditch merits inclusion as an Olympic sport.

Furthermore, if you're going to choose something false to give your life meaning or purpose, there are many more exciting choices than whatever religion your parents happened to practice. Why not the belief that the eight-year gap in your life starting in the mid-seventies was caused by aliens who abducted you and took you to the planet Phaelon and studied you and filled your head up with star charts in an attempt to demonstrate that humans only use 10% of their brains? Or the belief that you might have been brainwashed into becoming a killing machine by Chinese Communists in league with your mother, Angela Lansbury, during the Korean War? Or (especially) the belief that the new green variety of processed food-wafers from the Soylent Corporation are not made from high-energy algae at all, but are in fact made out of people?

Personally, I choose to look for meaning in beautiful, mundane events, and (with the revelation that your religion is false) I suggest that you do the same. In case you have trouble finding your purpose, here are some possibilities:

- Prove to Amy Fleming that she was a fool for breaking up with me
- Get the high score on the Galaga machine at the bowling alley

- Read all the books in the *Sweet Valley High* and *Sweet Valley Twins* series
- Use every restroom in every major league baseball stadium
- Finish writing anti-religious polemic
- Try every flavor of Jelly Bellies
- Sing "Don't Stop Believing" at karaoke
- Learn to say "duty" without giggling
- Get to spin the big wheel on "Price is Right"
- Meet Morrissey without crying

88

Religious freedom and religious tolerance

History teems with examples of people who've been persecuted on the basis of their religion. Hitler killed millions of Jews just for being Jews; the Romans used to feed Christians to lions (who, according to zookeepers, much prefer Zoroastrians); Iran tortures and executes its Bahá'í; China forcibly re-educates the Falun Gong.

Similarly, religions often seek to exterminate each other. The Catholics and the Muslims fought a bitter series of Crusades during the Middle Ages; Hindus and Muslims are perpetually at war in India; Jews and Muslims have been killing each other in the Middle East since Judaism and Islam were invented.

In response to these events, a mix of the opportunistic and the naively kind-hearted have agitated for the dual importance of (the despicable ideas of) "religious freedom" and "religious tolerance."

religious freedom: the idea that I should be allowed to shirk my job responsibilities and to do things that are illegal (or questionably legal, or perhaps just distasteful), as long as I claim a "religious" reason for doing so

religious tolerance: the idea that nobody should be allowed to criticize my choices and beliefs, as long I claim them to be "religious"

Every morning the news is full of stories about the Orthodox Jew beer vendor who refuses (on religious grounds) to take his hat off during the traditional seventh-inning-stretch singing of "Take Me Out to the Ballgame," the Muslim cab driver who refuses (on religious grounds) to transport passengers traveling with pot-bellied pigs, the Christian-Scientist pharmacist who refuses (on religious grounds) to dispense any medications, and the Objectivist inventor who refuses (on religious grounds) to grant licenses for his new super-strong metallic alloy. Normally, when someone refuses to do his job, we fire him. But the religious freedom crowd insists that when someone refuses to his job for religious reasons, we should instead celebrate him!

And the religious tolerance crowd is even worse! They would (if they had their way) make it illegal to point out simple truths like "god isn't real" and "Mohammed was a pedophile" and "Jesus ran a meth lab" and "L. Ron Hubbard liked to ▮▮ ▮▮ with his ▮▮▮." They think it should be a crime to draw unflattering cartoons of Ahura Mazda, to erect a billboard reading "Haredi Jews do it religiously," to download the latest Eric Clapton album off the internet, to criticize Thomas Kinkade's business practices, or to write a negative review of Malcolm X (e.g. "Never quite bitchy enough to be enjoyable" or "The funniest moments are all in the trailer"). They are so unconfident in their beliefs, so fearful of criticism, so opposed to free speech that they want the force of law to apply to those who question them, to those who mock them, and to those who point out that their religions are false.

Now, just to stave off accusations to the contrary, I do not think people should be killed or punished for their dumb religious choices. People like Hitler, who killed millions of people for practicing the wrong religion, are just as evil as the Popes, who killed millions of people for not practicing the right religion; just as evil as Che Guevara, who killed millions of people so he could get his face on a t-shirt; and just as evil as Hannibal Lecter, who killed millions of people so he could eat their innards paired with fava beans and a nice Chianti.

Nonetheless, it should be perfectly clear at this point in the book that we (that's you and I, dear reader) have no tolerance for and owe no tolerance to people who believe stupid things. This world would be a much more pleasant place if more people would follow our examples. And so, when you buy an extra dozen copies of this book to hand out to your friends and loved ones who've been secretly yearning for the "your religion is false" message (go ahead, purchase them now, I'll wait), you might want to add a handwritten note letting them know how much you care. Here is a sample that you are welcome to use:

> My Dearest Geraldine,
>
>   I take my pen in hand to inform you that I am well at present and hope these few lines may find you and the children and all of the rest of the folks well. Our regiment just got in yesterday from Lebanon, Tenn. where they had a desperate fight with a body of rebels under a notorious Ky. robber by the name of Morgan. The rebels were about 800 strong while ours did not amount to more than 600. But our boys whipped them badly, killing seventy odd and took 200 prisoners, 155 horses, 180 stand of arms and chased

the balance of them 18 miles. You must write as soon as you get this and write every week if you can for I am half crazy if I don't get a letter every week. Take good care of yourself and the children and kiss them all for me. I never go to sleep without thinking of you and them. So nothing more at present but remaining your affectionate husband until death, because your religion (which promises life after death) is false.

J.S. Grus

You should probably use your name for the signature, though.

89

Separation of church and state

In the past, there was often no division between a country's religion and its government. The Ottoman Empire was an explicitly Muslim state; the Holy Roman Empire was Catholic; Japan was Shinto; Zoroastria was Zoroastrian; and Giant-Stone-Head-Worship-Land was devoted to the worship of giant stone heads.

In the last few hundred years, however, political reformers have made a number of brave attempts at creating non-religious governments. The United States of America is nominally a secular country, despite references to god on its fiat money, the words "under god" in its Loyalty Pledge, the routine presence of religious prayers at the commencement of legislative sessions and Presidential terms, frequent religious displays on government property at Christmas-time, the widespread use of religious oaths to swear in jurors, government funding and endorsement of "faith-based programs," routine attempts to include creationism in public school curricula, requirements for state-level elected officials to profess belief in a supreme being, official religious chaplains for government functions, and government support of organizations that refuse membership to atheists.

As mentioned earlier, this separation is often used to give religious people the religious freedom to do things that would be prohibited to non-religious people. Amerindians can smoke peyote, while you and I cannot. Amish can opt out of the Social Security system, while the rest of us are forced to fund the extravagant lifestyles of octogenarians. Religious groups receiving federal funds are allowed to discriminate in employment in ways that other groups receiving federal funds may not. Sikhs are often allowed to carry daggers in places where you and I would be arrested for bringing a weapon.

Don't get me wrong – you should feel fortunate that constitutional restrictions have (so far) been interpreted to prevent the establishment of a state religion, that no one besides your parents is allowed to tell you what you have to believe, and that we have a political system in which it is possible for admitted atheists to receive as much as 15% of the votes in certain elections.

Nonetheless, as long as religious trappings remain integral parts of our government and religious people and groups are given special privileges denied to the rest of us, "separation of church and state" is a bit of a misnomer.

90

Hot-button issues, A to Z

Having slogged our way through the details of every religion imaginable, we are now finally equipped to discuss the issues that religious types get themselves so worked up over.

Abortion

To some people (Catholics especially), abortion represents the abhorrent termination of a pregnancy by killing and removing the fetus. To others (for example, Environmentalists), abortion is merely the termination of a pregnancy by killing and removing the fetus. Liberal Protestants often believe that abortion should be safe, legal, and rare, while some of the more extreme Wiccans (for instance) argue that abortion should be dangerous, illegal, and common. If there is a common ground here, I'm not seeing it.

Books about Wizard Academies

Christians often get upset about these books, fearing that they promote witchcraft, which they consider a less reasonable thing to believe in than resurrection and virgin births and trinitarianism. In return, Wiccans tend to get upset about Christian literature, mostly because it tends to be poorly written, with tin-eared dialogue and pacing problems.

Corporal Punishment

It's in the Bible:

> He who spares the rod hates his son, but he who loves him is careful to discipline him.

Proverbs 13:24

However, some people believe that this is in fact a command to take your kid fishing.

Death Penalty

Most religions (with the notable exception of People's Temple) contain nominal prohibitions on killing. At the same time, most religions (with the notable exception of Jainism) explicitly endorse the retributive "eye-for-an-eye" killings of kidnappers, sodomites, gomorrons, false prophets, traitors, hired assassins, apostates, and adulterers. This allows both religious proponents of the death penalty and religious opponents of the death penalty to confidently assert that god is on their side.

Evolution

Obviously, evolutionary biology is tough to reconcile with a dogma that asserts that god created all the creatures in the world over a seven day span, let alone with a dogma that asserts that Earth Mother vomited the universe during a bout of morning sickness or a dogma that asserts that our entire universe is actually an atom inside some cosmic giant's toenail.

However, the Catholic Church (as one example) steadfastly maintains that evolutionary theory and its religious pronouncements are not in conflict, which indeed they are not as long as you don't try to think about them at the same time. In recent years, some rogue theologians *have* tried to think about them at the same time and have accordingly adopted skepticism toward evolutionary theory (but for some reason not toward god the holy spirit).

Fantasy Role-Playing Games

Most religions (the two exceptions that come to mind are Jediism and Dungeons and Dragons) frown on games that immerse players in magical worlds, typically based on the argument that exposure to the sorts of magic that everyone agrees don't really exist might cause people to disbelieve in the sorts of magic that their religions teach *do* really exist. Groups such as MADD (Muslims Against Dungeons and Dragons) and AARP (Anglicans Against Role Playing) have accordingly created boring anti-fantasy essays, like "Should a Zoroastrian Play Dungeons and Dragons?" and boring anti-fantasy movies, like *Mazes and Monsters*, and boring anti-fantasy television channels, like "C-SPAN2."

Genital Mutilation

Ever since god told Abraham to cut off the tip of his wiener, religious people have merrily subjected their children to a panoply of genital mutilation,

including circumcision, clitoridectomy, excision, infibulation, oophorec-
tomy, cauterization, hymenorrhaphy, ampallangs, labia-stretching, gishiri,
needle-pricking, dolphin-piercing, subincision, breast-ironing, meato-
tomy, pearling, vulvectomy, gompco-clamping, plastibelling, frenulec-
tomy, gukuna imishino, preputioplasty, and Prince Alberts. Although
the original justification was always some version of "to perfect what is
defective morally," these days pro-mutilation advocates tend to gloss over
the pleasure-killing aspect and are more likely to argue "it will save him
from being embarrassed in the locker room," "we want her to look like
her mom down there," "it will help prevent HIV transmission in the event
he starts having sex with intravenous drug users," or "it's my kid, I can do
what I want to it."

Human Cloning

Whether it's the Raëlians (who consider cloning "the first step toward
human immortality"), the Catholics (who call for "a complete and explicit
prohibition of all techniques of creating new individual human embryos
by cloning"), the Jedis (who fear a repeat of the Republic-destroying Clone
Wars), the Muslims (who worry that a human clone would invalidate the
"only Allah can create a human being" plank of their religion, causing
the whole edifice to crumble), or the Second Coming Project (who spent
most of 1999 unsuccessfully trying to clone Jesus), all religions seem to
have an opinion on cloning. Unfortunately, all these opinions are wrong.
Cloning is awesome primarily because it will allow every household to
have its own Elvis.

Interfaith

Once upon a time, people were strongly discouraged from socializing
with believers in other religions. They worked with, lived next to, played
little league with, dated, and married pretty much exclusively their co-
religionists. In recent years the internet has broken down many of these
barriers, and now it is not uncommon to find a Muslim working for a
Zoroastrian, a Reform Jew living next to a Jain, a Rasta turning double
plays with a Mormon and a Pantheist, a Hellenic Polytheistic Reconstruc-
tionist taking a Wiccan to the prom, and a Catholic marrying a Giant
Stone Head Worshipper.

    But no matter how much our public education system drums the
"virtues" of tolerance into little children's heads, conflicts are bound to
occur. "Should we put up a Christmas tree, a Chanukah bush, a Kwanzaa

plant, or a Ramadan topiary?" "How come I always have to be the Birdman?" "I know you're *supposed* to get eaten by vultures after you die, but I think that would really traumatize the children!"

If there is an upside, it's that repeated close-up exposure to multiple religions can (especially if supplemented with gift copies of this book) speed people down the path of realizing their religions are false.

Jokes About Golf-Playing Clergymen

A Catholic priest, an Orthodox priest, a Protestant minister, a Reform rabbi, a Buddhist monk, a Wiccan coven leader, a Hellenist oracle, a Hindu priest, a Caodaist giáo tông, a Zoroastrian gabr, an African shaman, a Muslim imam, a Scientologist OT VII, a Cherokee chief, a Sikh guru, a Jain jina, a Falun Gong practitioner, a Sufi mystic, a Shinto kami, a Jedi knight, a Voodoo zombie, a Rasta ras, an Objectivist philosopher, a Mormon elder, a Level 18 cleric, a Pastafarian pirate, and an atheist are playing golf.

These clergymen are getting bogies and double bogies and triple bogies, but the guy playing in front of them keeps getting holes in one.

So the Catholic priest says, "Who does that guy think he is, the Pope?" And the Orthodox priest says, "Who does that guy think he is, the Patriarch of Constantinople?" And the minister says, "Who does that guy think he is, Jesus Christ?" And the rabbi says, "Who does that guy think he is, Moses?" And the monk says, "Who does that guy think he is, the Buddha?" And the coven leader says, "Who does that guy think he is, Harry Potter?" And the oracle says, "Who does that guy think he is, Achilles?" And the Hindu priest says, "Who does that guy think he is, Vishnu?" And the giáo tông says, "Who does that guy think he is, Cao Đài Tiên Ông Đại Bồ Tát Ma-ha-tát?" And the gabr says, "Who does that guy think he is, Zoroaster?" And the shaman says, "Who does that guy think he is, Tikoloshe?" And the imam says, "Who does that guy think he is, Mohammed?" And the OT VII says, "Who does that guy think he is, David Miscavige?" And the chief says, "Who does that guy think he is, Great Spirit?" And the guru says, "Who does that guy think he is, Nanak Dev?" And the jina says, "Who does that guy think he is, Shri Mahavir?" And the Gonger says, "Who does that guy think he is, Li Hongzhi?" And the mystic says, "Who does that guy think he is, Uwais al-Qarni?" And the *kami* says, "Who does that guy think he is, Amaterasu-omikami"? And the Jedi says, "Who does that guy think he is, Yoda?" And the zombie says, "Who does that guy think he is, Marie Laveau?" And the ras says, "Who does that guy think he is, Haile Selassie?"

And the Objectivist says, "Who does that guy think he is, Howard Roark?"
And the elder says, "Who does that guy think he is, Brigham Young?"
And the cleric says, "Who does that guy think he is, Garl Glittergold?"
And the pirate says, "Who does that guy think he is, the Flying Spaghetti Monster?"
So the atheist says, "No, that's Tiger Woods."

Killing Yourself

Some religions (for example, Heaven's Gate and People's Temple and Islam) look favorably on killing yourself, especially if you can manage to take a bunch of other people with you. Other religions (I'm looking at you, Catholicism) frown on the practice, arguing that only god the holy spirit (possibly acting through a drunk driver) gets to kill you, and that he'll torture you for eternity if you deprive him the pleasure.

Luckily for the clinically depressed, there is a middle ground, in that pretty much all religions promise great rewards for martyrdom, the act of taunting a non-believer until he snaps and kills you. The Catholics, who are totally, 100% against suicide, are at the same time 100% for "suicide-by-lion" if you manage to antagonize the non-Catholic emperor. (According to rumors on message boards, this was in fact the premise of Sylvia Plath's last, unfinished novel.)

License Plates with Religious Messages

In a number of states, drivers are given the option to proudly proclaim that they are not among the awful few percent of non-religious Americans by purchasing license plates with religious messages like "IN GOD WE TRUST" and "ONE NATION UNDER GOD" and "CHOOSE LIFE" (though it is possible that some fraction of those sporting the last plate are merely Andrew Ridgeley fans). Your humble author petitioned the DMV offices in several states for a corresponding "YOUR RELIGION IS FALSE" plate, but was placed at the end of a long queue of requests, behind "HAVE A HEART, HELP OUR KIDS," "ALPHA KAPPA ALPHA SORORITY" and "FAN OF GENERAL ROBERT E. LEE."

Masturbation

Many religions maintain that masturbation is "spiritually detrimental," which is hard to disagree with, since it doesn't mean anything. So what do you do when you're faced with the sometimes-overwhelming desire to lovingly caress yourself while mentally undressing Laura Leighton?

Religions typically suggest a variety of distractions including prayer, thinking about baseball, avoiding spicy foods, changing the channel when "Melrose Place" is on, duct-taping your pajamas shut, and only looking at yourself in mirrors when you're wearing clothes. Some religions (I'm looking at you, Ahura Mazda) further teach that masturbation can lead to blindness and hairy palms, while others grudgingly accept that masturbation is normal and merely insist that you refrain from using a Fleshlight, a Sybian, a Monkey Rocker, or cyberdildonics.

Nonviolence

On one hand, you have the Jains, who practice ahimsa. On the other hand, you have the Muslims, who practice suicide bombings. And in the middle you have everyone else.

Organ Donation

According to organdonor.gov, most religions encourage organ donation, either because it is an act of fraternal love, because the beloved Hindu god Ganesh owed his existence to a head-donating elephant, or because "the Pope has no objection at this time." A notable exception is Shinto, in which dead bodies are considered impure and dangerous and powerful and not-to-be-messed-with.

However, in the vanishingly unlikely event that Christ (or maybe some sort of alien visitor with unimaginable technologies) returns and brings the dead back to life, do you really want to be caught without your eyes, without your heart, or without your liver? It's something worth thinking about!

Prayer in Schools

Many religious people advocate that all schools provide organized prayer, either to acknowledge that the scientifically-illiterate people who founded the country hundreds of years ago believed in the importance of prayer, to teach kids that bullying is wrong (except when god does it), or to ferret out unbelievers and facilitate their persecution.

However, in many countries this sort of government-sponsored religion is illegal, forcing schools to replace prayer with either a moment of silence, morning announcements read by a popular kid over the intercom, "make-out minutes," Bellamy salutes, or pledges of unconditional allegiance to flags and governments.

Queers

Many religions condemn gays, lesbians, bisexuals, trannyboys, nancies, queers, fruits, fags, manhole-inspectors, tinkerbells, bug-chasers, cat-lappers, inverts, bean-flickers, dykes, friends of Dorothy, chubs, chicken-hawks, tailgunners, bean-queens, uphill-gardeners, rug-munchers, brownie-kings, pedicators, shemales, anal-bum-coverers, pillow-biters, slit-ninjas, fudge-packers, cunnilinctrices, wind-jammers, sissies, limp-wrists, quag-gots, carnivorous canaries, rump-rangers, vagitarians, fairy godmoth-ers, leather-daddies, rear-admirals, buggerers, colon-bowlers, twinks, butter-mouths, flamers, semi-diesels, stool-pushers, bone-smugglers, gerbil-crammers, and bum-chums.

Religious types persecuting these crevice-couriers typically carry signs like "It was Adam and Eve, not Adam and Steve," "Donut-Punching is a Sin," and "God Hates Clam-Smackers!" This leads to predictable hilarity each time one of the sign carriers is himself revealed to be a closeted chutney-ferret.

Of course, the primary message of this book is that there is no god to care about your brownpipe-engineering, so butt-pirate away!

Restimulation

A few religions (most notably ███████████) argue that restimulation repre-sents the ████████ of an ██████, "a mental ██████ picture of a moment of ████ and ████████████." Most other religions will tell you that ████ don't actually exist, and that what most people think of as "████████████" is simply god's way of sending messages to schizophrenics. Either way, it's a pretty nutty concept.

Slavery

Although slavery is today considered abhorrent by a slight majority of people, it was a popular working arrangement back in the days when most religions were invented. Accordingly, many religious scriptures endorse the practice. Exodus 21:21 suggests that it is acceptable to beat your slaves as long as they are disabled for no more than two days afterward. Ephesians 6:5 exhorts slaves to obey their masters in the exact same way they would obey a whip-wielding Jesus. Sura 23:6 grants that the believing Muslim is allowed sex slaves. And the *Rig Veda* allowed Hindus to take female slaves as spoils of war.

But as the tide of public sentiment turned against slavery, these same religions conveniently discovered that their scriptures also forbade the practice! And thanks to the tireless efforts of these reformers, slavery can nowadays only be found in Asia, Africa, and parts of Europe and Australia and South America.

Time Travel

Most religions oppose time travel. Christians worry primarily that time travelers might return with evidence that Jesus never existed. Intelligent-Design-believers fear photographs of "missing links" that will make their denial of evolutionary theory even more ludicrous than it is already. And Orthodox Jews wish to avoid having to reinterpret traditional creation stories to account for the existence of Morlocks and Eloi.

Pretty much the only religions supporting time travel are Singularitarianism (whose believers imagine that freezing their brains will effectively transport them into the future) and New Age (whose believers imagine that they can time travel via Astral Projection if they simply imagine a clock with its hands spinning rapidly forward or backward).

Urine-drinking

So what if the Prophet Mohammed liked to cool down with a frosty mug of camel urine at the end of the day? Who are you to judge?

Vouchers for Religious Schools

Many religious conservatives (of all religious persuasions) are not happy that their tax dollars are used to fund public schools that are nominally secular but that are largely run according to Environmentalist and New Age and Unitarian dogma. If these conservatives want to send their children to schools run instead according to Christian dogma or Muslim dogma or Zoroastrian dogma, they argue, why should they have to pay a second time? However, public-school-proponents insist this would violate separation of church and state, which (although enforced only sporadically) requires that government not endorse any religions other than Environmentalism and New Age and Intelligent Design.

One proposed solution is a system of vouchers that would transfer each student's portion of tax dollars to the school of his choice. Naturally, the Environmentalists and New Agers and Intelligent Designers who run the public schools object to the potential loss of both students and revenue. Another proposed solution is homeschooling, although this doesn't work for people who, for example, hate kids and think of school as "that blissful

6 hours each day when the house is quiet enough for me to drink wine and watch my stories."

Women Clergy

In most religions, the priesthood has traditionally been restricted to men. Catholics, for instance, teach that this is a requirement of "divine law," which is not altogether different from "because I said so," although a few dissidents argue that the church will soon run out of priests unless women start being ordained. Muslims typically teach that women may lead women-only congregations (like in the movie *Where the Boys Aren't #8*) but may not under any circumstances lead mixed-gender congregations (like in the movie *Chitty Chitty Gang Bang*). Orthodox Jews insist that only men may become rabbis, while Reform Jews actively encourage women to become rabbis. Most Protestants these days are happy to appoint women as televangelists, but only if they have huge, bird's-nest-like hair and wear grotesque amounts of clownish makeup.

XXX Movies

I know what you're thinking – how could anyone possibly be opposed to the artistic medium responsible for such classics as *A Clockwork Orgy, Add Momma To The Train, Beverly Hills Copulator, Big Trouble In Little Vagina, Children Of The Cornhole, The Dykes of Hazzard, Gleaming the Pube, Heavy Into Jeff, Inspect Her Gadget, Intercourse With The Vampire, The Loin King, Oh She's Eleven, Planet of the Gapes, Schindler's Fist, Shaving Ryan's Privates, Sorest Rump,* and *Womb Raider?*

Actors like Lexington Steele, a devout Baptist who was named AVN Male Performer of the Year an unprecedented three times, demonstrate that pornography and religion need not be mutually exclusive. Nonetheless, with the notable exception of Thelema, most religions take a dim view of pornography, typically arguing that it offends against chastity, titillates, perverts the conjugal act, destroys individuals and families like a raging storm, violates modesty requirements, immerses participants in a dreamlike fantasy world, allows women's ankles to be seen by male non-relatives, glorifies the naked human body, and reinforces cultural attitudes that are complicit in sexual harassment.

Your Religion Is False

Hopefully this is pretty clear by now.

Zooerasty

Except for the "First Church of Zoophilia" (which is mentioned in most of the articles about the dude who married his horse Pixel) and Shi'a Islam (whose Ayatollah Khomeini is supposed to have endorsed various forms of bestiality in his bestselling book *Tahrirolvasyleh*), most religions frown on zooerasty. Hinduism, for example, not only punishes inter-species sex but provides extra punishment in the all-too-common event that one of the participants is a sacred cow.

Conclusion

In conclusion, it doesn't matter how many birdman contests you win, how many bricks you put under your bed, how many oracles you consult, how many poles you carve, how many cows you worship, how much flax you weigh, how long you grow your hair, how few clothes you wear, how many corpses you feed to vultures, how much Esperanto you speak, how many times you rearrange your bedroom, how many deep belly massages you get, how many times you stand on a toilet, how many purification rituals you lead, how few cheeseburgers you eat, how many Madonna albums you own, how many crackers you eat, how many plates you break, how many theses you nail to doors, how many potlucks you organize, how many snakes you handle, how many cement blocks you smash, how many paintings you sell, how many pilgrimages you make to Mecca, how many cars you burn, how many bad poems you write, how many pamphlets you hand out, how many reading rooms you open, how many prizes you win, how many days you go without a drink, how many Veja-Links ® you eat, how many times your mouth is stuffed with dung, how little electricity you use, how many wives you have, how many midichlorians are in your blood, how often you listen to "Under the Bridge," how many zombies you create, how many spells you cast, how many lab animals you kidnap, how many needles you stick in your meridians, how many star charts you draw, how many patents you hold, how many ███████ you ██████████, how much Kool-aid you drink, how much science you mischaracterize, how many spinning balls of energy you rotate, how many PBS specials you have, how much weed you smoke, how many seer stones you use, how often you ride the bus, how many hit records you have, how many trolls you kill, how many novellas you write, how many matches you attend, how much bark you eat, how much pasta you worship, how many dinosaurs you sing along with, how many gods you believe in, how self-unaware you are, how mushy-headed your non-thinking is, or how little you care about anything.

Your religion is false. Have a nice day.

Acknowledgements

I am indebted to Jimbo Wales, whose Wikipedia project saved me from having to go to the library and talk to librarians and handle germy books. (In particular, the pages "Category:Lists of things considered unusual" and "List of scandals with '-gate' suffix" were invaluable.) Although the writing in this book is all mine, any factual errors are probably Wikipedia's. I hope Jimmy is not overly upset by the "Objectivism is false" chapter.

Michael Shermer suggested (in a very kind way) that I would never get this book published through a "reputable" publisher, which (after an evening of heavy drinking and feeling sad) I was able to channel as motivation to correct most of the spelling errors and also some of the more glaring grammatical mistakes. Also, as is almost always the case, he was right.

I am grateful to Sarah Hill, whose years of incessant attempts to share the "good news" about Jesus not only provided entertainment to our colleagues but also forced me to come up with a number of the arguments incorporated into this book. Along opposite lines I am grateful to Cesar Rebellon, with whom I (many, many years ago) first discussed many of these ideas.

I should also thank Noel Alumit, my first (and only) writing teacher, who was the first real live person (i.e. not an internet weirdo) to encourage my writing. I hope that in some small way this book makes up for me never finishing the short story about the kid who wants to play baseball but is no good at it.

Thanks, too, to the internet weirdos. You know who you are. Special thanks to John Perich, who read an early draft and commented that he liked the "Woody Allen / Manhattan / plagiarism" story, and to Kim Hamm, who reminded me about Nigel St. Hubbins.

The denizens of comp.text.tex offered useful advice that on several occasions prevented me from throwing my computer out the window.

During my Sufi Poetry phase, Jay Fundling suggested writing about "the man from Medina," which I am ashamed to admit I might not have thought of on my own. Around the same time, Jen Field helpfully pointed out that I had forgotten to include a chapter on Twelve-Step Programs.

I am grateful to the operators of the internet stations "Radio Free Akron" and "Radio Nigel," whose upbeat mixes of New Wave 1980's music provided the bulk of the soundtrack for my writing.

Above all, I owe thanks to Ganga Subramanian, whose repeated suggestions of "Why don't you stop swearing at Joel Osteen and work on your book instead?" were my principal source of encouragement throughout this project.

About the author

Joel Grus lives in Seattle.
He maintains a website at
http://yrif.org
and can be contacted at
your.religion.is.false@gmail.com

LaVergne, TN USA
05 October 2009
159849LV00004B/115/P